THE MEA[...] THE WARM[...]

THIRTEEN NEW TESTAMENT STUDIES OF BIBLICAL AND MODERN DISCIPLES

DONALD ENGLISH

Prepared under the direction of the World Methodist Council

Book Five in the
World Evangelism Library

DISCIPLESHIP RESOURCES

MATERIALS FOR GROWTH IN CHRISTIAN FAITH AND LIFE

P.O. Box 189 • Nashville, TN 37202 • Phone (615) 340-7285

Unless otherwise indicated, all scriptural references are taken from the New Testament in Today's English Version.

ISBN 0-88177-050-7

Library of Congress Catalog Card No. 87-50767

DR050B

For Paul

———————————

First, I wish to thank the People called Methodists for my Christian beginning and nurture, and for the context of my ministry. That is a debt I can never repay. I am grateful, too, to all those who have participated in the production of this book, particularly Discipleship Resources, and to those who will translate it into the variety of languages used by our World Methodist family. Finally, I offer my thanks to Mrs. Valerie Castle, who typed the manuscript with unfailing graciousness and encouragement.

World Evangelism Library

A World Evangelism Library has been established by the World Evangelism Committee of The World Methodist Council. From time to time, books will be published to explore and explain the meaning of evangelism. Behind the books which are added to the Library will be scholarly research and actual experience in the practice of evangelism. Each book will be a responsible expression of evangelical Christianity, discussing issues of vital concern to every Christian and the whole church. The Library aims to enlarge the resources of evangelism for every part of the church of Jesus Christ. The first five books of the Library are:

1. *The Mystery and Meaning of Christian Conversion* by George E. Morris, Associate Professor of Evangelism at Candler School of Theology, Atlanta, Georgia, and Director of the Institute for World Evangelism.
2. *Standing Up to Preach: The Art of Evangelical Preaching* by Alan Walker, Director of World Evangelism for The World Methodist Council.
3. *Rethinking Congregational Development* edited by George E. Morris.
4. *Faith-Sharing: Dynamic Christian Witnessing by Invitation* by George E. Morris and H. Eddie Fox.
5. *The Meaning of the Warmed Heart* by Donald English.

Contents

How to Use This Book

This is a book about how people become disciples of Jesus, and about what it means to be a disciple. The title comes from John Wesley's words describing the experience in Aldersgate Street, London, which changed the course of his life. He wrote, "I felt my heart strangely warmed."

Methodist scholars and preachers differ in their assessment of what John Wesley experienced on May 24th, 1738. Traditionally the warmed heart is seen as his conversion. Others see it as an experience of assurance of faith; still others as fullness of the Spirit; yet others as the completion of something which began years earlier. These interpretations vary, partly according to the theology of the interpreter and partly in line with how he or she became and remains a disciple. Whatever one says about what happened to John Wesley, it certainly shows that Methodists have a variety of understandings of what it means to be a disciple and a variety of experiences of how one becomes a disciple.

This book does not attempt to answer the question about John Wesley and Aldersgate. Many learned writers have already done that. Here we look at a variety of New Testament stories about how people became and remained disciples of Jesus. We examine the theological issues arising from the stories, looking particularly at their relevance to Methodist history and doctrine. Finally in each case some lessons are indicated about our discipleship and mission today. And there is a story in each chapter of a contemporary disciple whose experience relates to the biblical passage being studied.

The basic theme is the New Testament evidence of a variety of ways in which people become disciples of Jesus and behave as his disciples. Our way of becoming a disciple must not narrow down our vision of how to be one. To use a picture, becoming a Christian disciple is not going through a door into a tunnel, mutually exclusive of all other doors or tunnels. It is rather to go through a gate into an arena, an arena which reveals that there are many other ways into discipleship through Jesus than the one we followed; and many other perceptions of being a disciple than ours. Part of Christian growth involves enlarging our perception and appreciation of these other gates which all go through Jesus Christ into this large arena. In this Bible study we will discover how Scripture supports this diversity.

This is a study book, for individuals, groups, or congregations. Part One of the book is particularly suitable during Lent, but the book can be adapted to any length of Bible study that you wish. Since it is written for Methodist readers all over the world, it will need translating culturally as well as linguistically. Preachers, teachers, group or class leaders will need to do this for their people. Sometimes a Scripture reference is given; often the readers are left to test out the points made by searching the set passage for themselves. Where groups use the study, they are invited to share their own personal experiences as stimulated by the Bible text and the comment in this book.

Readers are invited to allow the story of Jesus to engage their own story so that all our hearts may be warmed by the gospel.

1
NATHANIEL
John 1:43-50

Nathaniel is one of the less well-known persons in the Gospels. He comes and goes briefly at the beginning of John's Gospel, when the writer is describing a number of encounters between Jesus and people whom he called to follow him.

What kind of person was Nathaniel? Nathaniel was probably rather shy. We picture him as one being approached by others rather than taking the initiative himself. He seems to have been a cautious person, too. John's Gospel suggests that he is keeping close enough to Jesus to observe what he is doing and to hear what he is saying, yet he is not in the crowd. He is under a tree, watching and listening from a distance. Was he, one wonders, both envious and critical of people like Simon Peter, always at the front of the crowd and always having something ready to say? Whatever he thought about aggressive people, he certainly was not like them.

If he was shy and cautious, however, he did not lack interest in what Jesus was teaching. Not everyone shows interest by pushing to the front and talking. He was not only interested, as his response to Philip's invitation shows, but he also had reflected on these matters. When Philip claimed that they had found the Messiah promised in Hebrew Scriptures, and that he came from Nazareth, Nathaniel was quick to question whether such a Messiah was at all likely. He was going to be no "push-over." He was a serious, reflective person, interested in truth, needing evidence before committing himself. Confident claims by others were not in themselves adequate evidence for him.

1

How did Nathaniel become a disciple? As so often in Christian witness, a friend made contact and offered an invitation. Research by one denomination in the United States of America revealed that 80 percent of people joining the church gave as their main reason for doing so the influence upon their lives of family, friends, neighbors, and colleagues at work. In this story it was Philip who shared with his friend Nathaniel what he had discovered about Jesus.

It was in Philip's company that Nathaniel drew nearer to Jesus. He was probably totally unprepared for what happened next. Rather than Nathaniel telling Jesus who he was, Jesus told Nathaniel who Nathaniel was! The dialogue which follows suggests that Jesus was aware of Nathaniel long before Nathaniel realized it. He had seen him "under the fig tree, before Philip called you." In spite of whatever else was happening, Jesus had noticed him. What is more, he evidently perceived things about him. "Here is a real Israelite: there is nothing false in him." There is both irony and humor in this statement. The irony is that in the Hebrew Scriptures Jacob is often referred to as Israel, and Jacob was full of guile! The humor lay in Jesus' way of praising Nathaniel's quality by means of a subtle historical pun.

The effect on Nathaniel was dramatic. When he had thought himself to be well concealed, he had actually been noticed by Jesus. When he plucked up courage to find out more about this rabbi, he discovered that the rabbi knew all about him. Yet it is all done with such warmth and humor, and in a way which expects him to be informed and responsive, that he cannot take offense.

We now discover how deeply Nathaniel had reflected on religious matters, and how ready he was to be a disciple. "Teacher," he says to Jesus, "you are the Son of God! You are the King of Israel." We may feel that he had not heard much on which to base such a commitment. Evidently Jesus' approach to him, and the conversation between them, was enough to reach the depths of Nathaniel's being and evoke response. He had discovered enough to take the step into discipleship. He would have much yet to learn, but the crucial step had been taken. He made his public affirmation.

Jesus, too, seemed to be aware of how much still lay in the future. Again he gently teased Nathaniel about it. "Do you believe just because I told you I saw you when you were under the fig tree? You will see much greater things than this!" A beginning has been made. There is much more to come.

What theological insights help us to make sense of Nathaniel's story? In many ways we are looking at a dramatic presentation of a Christian doctrine which John Wesley emphasized, the doctrine of "prevenient grace" (grace which comes before). Wesley sought to avoid two errors in the theological traditions which he saw around him. One was a popular Roman Catholic view of salvation which attached so much importance to what people must do that salvation seemed to depend on human works more than divine grace. The other was a popular Calvinistic view of salvation which attached so much importance to God's sovereign power and will that salvation seemed to leave no room for human involvement. Wesley's understanding of God's grace was too strong to allow him to accept the former view. Yet his understanding of both human dignity and the integrity of persons made in the image of God was too deep to allow him to accept the second view.

"Prevenient grace" bridged the chasm between the two views. God, by the Holy Spirit, is at work wherever the gospel is made known. By the Holy Spirit God makes a positive response possible at each step of the way. God makes it possible but doesn't enforce it. Each human response to God's grace is therefore truly that person's own response. We are not objects of divine manipulation. Yet we can only make such a response because God's prevenient grace has made it possible. If we respond positively and are saved, we have no credit to claim for ourselves. Our response was only possible because of God's grace. If we reject and are lost, however, we have nothing to complain about. God's prevenient grace made a positive response possible. The mystery remains of why some persons choose one way and others another way, but it is a mystery at the heart of the relationship between God and humanity. That is preferable to a solution depending upon an arbitrary God or an autonomous human race, neither of which meets the evidence around us.

The story of Nathaniel is almost a slow-motion portrayal of prevenient grace at work. God's grace has been at work in the quiet reflecting Nathaniel has done before our story begins. This is evident from the quality of his responses in the story. That grace continues to work: the approach by Philip, Philip's response to Nathaniel's question about Nazareth, the initial approach of Jesus, and the more detailed statement about Nathaniel. It is also there in Jesus' final promise that Nathaniel will see much more before he is finished. At each stage Nathaniel's response is an authentic expression of his understanding and desire to discover more. In the interplay of divine grace and divinely assisted human response, the pattern of Nathaniel's salvation unfolds.

What are we to learn from Nathaniel's story? To understand what true discipleship means, about both becoming and remaining a Christian, we learn from this story that we do better to concentrate on the interaction of prevenient grace and human response than to have one pattern of conversion which we seek to impose on everyone. Prevenient grace begins where we are. Since people are in different conditions, this means that there will be many patterns of conversion, determined as much by human conditions as by divine grace.

It may be that some of us will identify closely with Nathaniel's experience and find a reflection of it in our own. Or we may recognize in this story elements which help us to understand fellow-Christians who are different from us. We may even be helped by Nathaniel's story to understand some of our friends who are not yet Christians, and to perceive how we could help them toward faith, as Philip helped Nathaniel.

Above all, there is certainly the need for us to have a much deeper sense in our Christian mission that we are wholly dependent on God's prevenient grace in our witness and in our own discipleship.

1. What, in your view, is essential to your Christian confession of God's grace? What first made it possible for you to say that Jesus is the Son of God?

2. How do you tell if a person is a Christian or not? Is it your role to make such judgments?

3. What differences can you accept in the ways that people become Christians?

NNENE

Nnene was a Nigerian schoolteacher from a Methodist home. After university training she soon became the youngest headmistress in Eastern Nigeria. Some of the girls in her school sought and received permission to go to a Scripture Union holiday camp. Not being certain of what happened there, Nnene asked for a place too. The theme of the study periods was the Holy Spirit. As Nnene listened, she found herself less concerned to check what the girls were hearing. She felt she was herself being addressed by God. After one of the sessions, she gave her life to Christ. During the Biafran war she made a powerful witness to Christ.

2
NICODEMUS
John 3:1-13

Nicodemus appears in John's Gospel at a number of places. Mostly he is part of a larger story, as when he counsels his fellow Jewish leaders to be cautious about condemning Jesus without hearing him (John 7:50-51). Later, when Joseph of Arimathea gains permission to take Jesus' body for burial, we learn that Nicodemus goes with him and provides the necessary spices for the proper burial procedure, which he and Joseph dutifully follow (John 19:39-42). These two passages are important for our proper understanding of Nicodemus.

We learn most about him, however, in the section of John's Gospel which describes his private meeting with Jesus. (There is some doubt about whether John records the conversation as going on to verse 21 of John 3, but we limit ourselves here to verses 1-13 because it is these which tell us about Nicodemus).

What kind of a person was Nicodemus? John tells us that he was a Jewish leader, and this is borne out by the reference to him in John 7:45-52 where the chief priests and Pharisees are engaged in discussion about how to silence Jesus. Nicodemus was a Pharisee. The Pharisees were a Jewish religious party who were strict in their obedience to the Law of Moses and to the religious teaching and traditions which had grown up over the two centuries as additions to that Law. They wanted all Jews to practice the same. He was plainly a learned man, since he is referred to as a teacher of the law. Religion was a subject about which he knew a great deal.

His inquiring mind would not let him rest, however, when he

6

heard about (or witnessed personally) what Jesus said and did. As a Pharisee he ought to have opposed much of this, because Jesus was claiming to do things only God could do, such as forgiving sins. And Jesus was teaching things only God could teach, such as his additions to the law in the Sermon on the Mount. Yet Nicodemus recognized in what Jesus did the mark of God's blessing. He said so when he came to see Jesus by night. "No one could perform the mighty works you are doing unless God were with him." He is open to recognize as a servant of God someone whose teaching contradicts his own.

Was he a brave person or a cowardly one? He came by night to see Jesus. In John 7 he does not commit himself to support Jesus. He only cautions against condemning him without a hearing. In John 19 he was simply the helper of Joseph of Arimathea in collecting and burying the body of Jesus. All of this might suggest lack of courage. Yet he *did* go to see Jesus. No other Pharisee is recorded as doing so individually. Nor did anyone else defend Jesus' right to justice when the Jewish leaders were condemning him. And the act of sharing the burial certainly would make his position known. Was he then a naturally cautious man who was being as brave as he knew how, in those particular circumstances?

How did Nicodemus become a disciple? The conversation recorded in John 3 shows that he had personal experience of Jesus' ministry, or had heard reliable reports about it. He is willing to acknowledge that God is with Jesus. He particularly refers to the things Jesus did. Maybe Nicodemus had great doubts about Jesus' teaching but felt he could not ignore the evidence of what he did. Miracles come from God.

The story is not clear about why Nicodemus had come to talk with Jesus. He spoke of the miracles and what they represented. Jesus virtually ignored this and turned the conversation to the heart of the issue, how a person can belong to the kingdom of God.

It is a matter of being born again, or born from above. The word Jesus used really means a new beginning, and is used like this in regard to horticulture, when a new species is evolved, or in history when some new era begins. He is saying that entry into the kingdom requires an equivalent change in the life of an individual.

Although the word can mean *born again* or *born from above*, Nicodemus seems to have taken the former meaning, since he asks how a person who is fully grown can return to the womb. Jesus' reply suggests that Nicodemus is being too literal in interpreting his words. For all his great learning about the law, or because of it, he had missed the need for an inner spiritual change if one is to enter the kingdom of God. "A (person) is born physically of human parents, but . . . is born spiritually of the Spirit" (John 3:6). It will not be in keeping God's law that we will be saved but in receiving the Spirit's gift of inner renewal. You cannot see the Spirit any more than you can see the wind, but as with the wind you can see signs of the Spirit's presence.

Nicodemus is clearly unwilling to accept this. "How can this be?" (v. 9). He receives a rebuke from Jesus. He is a teacher, but he refuses to learn something from others who know. His commitment to what he teaches is preventing him from properly hearing the testimony of those who have discovered something new. If Nicodemus will not accept Jesus' witness about what needs to happen here, how can he ever learn about the hereafter? (v. 12).

This conversation, and especially the rebuke to Nicodemus, raises one important question which probably occurred to Nicodemus too. Who is this young person who presumes to lecture a teacher of the law about religious issues?

Jesus deals with that question in a roundabout way. Authority to teach about heavenly matters is possessed only by anyone who has been to heaven. But who has been to heaven? Jesus reminds Nicodemus of the figure of the Son of Man, featured particularly in Daniel 7:13-14. He is God's chosen one who has everlasting authority over God's kingdom. *Son of Man* is the description Jesus used again and again when describing or defending his own ministry.

Here he uses this description with considerable subtlety. He does not claim to be the Son of Man from heaven. Yet he answers a question about his right to teach about heaven by referring to the only one who could teach with such authority: the Son of Man. He leaves it to Nicodemus' subtle mind to draw the appropriate conclusion.

The other reference to Nicodemus in John's Gospel (chapters 7 and 19) traces significant steps in his response to this discussion in chapter 3. In 7:52 he is virtually accused of being a disciple of Jesus because he defends his right to a fair hearing. "Are you also from Galilee?" he was asked. In 19:39-42 he declares himself publicly by preparing Jesus' body for burial. It seems that John intends for us to conclude that in Nicodemus' case it was the things Jesus did which aroused his interest, but that he needed also the teaching about new birth as crucial to the meaning of the kingdom. Further, he needed time to observe and reflect before he was ready for a public declaration of discipleship.

What theological insights are raised by Nicodemus' story? First there is the fact that Jesus' actions could convince Nicodemus that God was with him. It is the fleshing out of faith which first encourages people to believe or discourages them from doing so. The understanding of Jesus as the incarnation of God carries with it the strong emphasis on demonstrating spiritual reality by bodily action. Spirit should not be separated from body so that what happens in the one is not reflected in the other. Again and again in the New Testament story of the growth of the early church, it was the things that Christians *did* which prepared the way for what they wanted to say. As Dr. John Stott has put it, "Presence must precede proclamation." Actions must happen before words. It is no coincidence that when people made extravagant spiritual claims to John Wesley, his reply was to request information about the "evidences." The kinds of lives we live are accurate reflections of our spiritual state. They are also powerful influences on others in their approach to or retreat from the kingdom of God.

The second theological issue raised concerns Nicodemus' reference to the miracles which Jesus did. It was not simply that Jesus was an impressive person or teacher. More important, the things he did revealed the presence of divine power in his life. It was this which Nicodemus could not gainsay.

This part of Christian experience is receiving new emphasis in many parts of the world in connection with "signs and wonders." On the one hand we must remember that the presence of divine power in the lives of God's people has always been an authentic part of Christian witness. Where it is lacking we can hardly expect others to be interested. On the other hand, demonstrations of supernatural power in the lives of believers are signs, not the reality. A traveler who confuses the signposts with the destination is not likely to arrive. Too much emphasis on the miraculous sign can distract attention from the truth of the gospel itself. John Wesley may sometimes have been too slow to welcome the unusual occurrences surrounding the preaching of the gospel, but his cautious instinct in the interest of preserving thoughtful concentration on the content of the gospel was surely right.

The third theological point concerns the new birth. It is sad that the description "born-again Christian" is now applied to particular groups in America. In biblical terms all Christians are born again, since there is no Christian faith without the inner operation of the Holy Spirit in human life. It is the Holy Spirit who makes the risen Christ a reality, and who enables us to understand the implications of the gospel in our lives. The words of Jesus in John 3 make this abundantly clear.

What are we to learn from Nicodemus' story? We can hardly exaggerate the importance of our individual and corporate lives as the influence which creates interest in the gospel. Equally important is our stress on the new birth as the heart of Christian experience. And there is the patience with which people like Nicodemus make their way to faith. Questions must be asked and answered on such a journey. Experiences must be reflected upon and conclusions reached. We must not rush ahead of the *patient urgency* of the Spirit's action in the life of another person. New birth, like physical birth, takes time.

1. Do you see your confession of Jesus as "new birth"?

2. What individual influenced you the most to become a Christian? How? What influences now help you most to grow as a Christian?

3. What group (church, study group, etc.) influenced you the most to become a disciple of Jesus? How? Which groups now help you most to grow as a disciple of Jesus?

NARAYAN

Narayan is a consultant neurosurgeon in India. He was raised in a Hindu family, and he did well in his medical studies. He came to Britain for advanced training. At a cocktail party in a university city where he studied, a Christian nurse noticed that he, almost alone in the room apart from her, was drinking orange juice instead of alcohol! She wrongly assumed that he was a Christian. She crossed the room and spoke to him. The effect on Narayan was totally unexpected. He said that when she spoke of her faith in Christ he knew he could tie her in knots philosophically and theologically. He was well versed in Hindu scriptures. But her deep personal commitment to Christ, and her conviction that he was alive today, disturbed and impressed the young Indian doctor very deeply.

As a result of that encounter he obtained a Bible and began to read it. The result was dramatic. His eyes were opened to see Jesus as the Son of God who died for Narayan and all human beings. The young doctor surrendered his life to Christ. When he returned home his family rejected him, former patients stoned his car, and the authorities put him into a mental institution. There, in his loneliness, he experienced Christ at a much deeper level. He studied his Bible incessantly and found his faith steadily deepened. He was discharged, and one by one his family were converted. He now works in a former mission hospital and travels the world witnessing for Christ.

3
THE WOMAN AT THE WELL
John 4:5-30, 39-41

So far in our studies we have seen Jesus dealing with people who were acceptable to the Jewish society of his day: Nathaniel, a distant seeker, and Nicodemus, a learned enquirer. If Jesus had met only people of this kind he would undoubtedly have had disagreements, but he would not have shocked and offended people. The story in this chapter begins to show the other side of his ministry—his willingness to mix with and talk to the unacceptable people in society. The so-called woman at the well is one such person.

Jesus in this case did not seek the woman out. She found him. And yet, by his willingness to wait all alone at a well, genuinely needing a drink, he made himself vulnerable to this kind of contact.

Who was the woman at the well? We know that she was a Samaritan (John 4:9). "You are a Jew and I am a Samaritan," she said to Jesus. Samaritans were natives of Samaria, the region between Judaea and Galilee. Because of differences going back over centuries, especially about religious belief and practice, there was a lot of bad feeling between Jews and Samaritans. We can guess that she was living immorally by the standards of faith and practice in her culture (John 4:17-18). "You are right when you say you don't have a husband," said Jesus. "You have been married to five men, and the man you live with now is not really your husband." As a result she appears to have been treated as an outcast by the other women of her neighborhood (John 4:7). As far as we can tell, she came alone for water, a dangerous and unusual thing to do. It is more likely that the other women simply would not come for water with an immoral woman.

What kind of person was the woman at the well? However lacking she was in conformity to the sexual morality of her time and culture, she had nevertheless reflected deeply on many serious issues, as the unfolding conversation reveals.

She was sensitive to the religious, cultural, and moral boundaries which Jesus crossed when he asked her for some water (John 4:7). Her reply is full of surprise and perception. "You are a Jew and I am a Samaritan—how can you ask me for a drink?" John 4:9 adds a word of explanation. "(Jews will not use the same cups and bowls that Samaritans use.)" She was sensitive and thoughtful enough to know how appalling this action of Jesus would be considered by Jews and Samaritans alike. Jews did not deal openly with Samaritans. Jewish men did not openly associate with women of any kind in this way.

She knew some history and some theology, too. When Jesus surprised her again by making hidden references to his own importance, she reminded him that Jacob (ancestor to both Jews and Samaritans) had given the local Samaritans that well. Did Jesus consider himself to be more important than Jacob, the renowned Israelite? (John 4:12). When Jesus disturbed her composure by revealing that he knew about her immoral life, she was able to turn to history and theology again with a question about where the place was for true worship of God, where they were now, or at Jerusalem where the temple was (John 4:20). Her theological grasp is even deeper than that, however. When Jesus speaks of the expected time (John 4:23) when all will be free to worship God everywhere, the woman immediately picks up his argument and develops it in terms of the Messiah, the anointed one, of God. "I know that the Messiah, called Christ, will come. When he comes he will tell us everything" (John 4:25).

If her neighbors concluded that she had no depth to her because her sexual behavior was loose, then they were sadly mistaken. Had she, however wrongly, decided to break outward rules because she perceived that much deeper issues were at stake, deeper issues of which the respectable law keepers were barely aware? Or had the fact of her wrongdoing, and the ignominy it brought her, caused her in her loneliness to reflect deeply on religion, on cultural values, and on her history as a Samaritan? Either way she was deeper than she seemed to be.

More than that, she had spiritual desires, too. When Jesus, in the course of the conversation, offers her water which will become an inner spring, providing life-giving water of eternal life, her response is immediate and urgent. "Sir, give me this water!" (John 4:15). The rest of her sentence shows that she hadn't yet penetrated to the depths of Jesus' picture-language, but whatever this miraculous water was, she wanted it. This is equally demonstrated by the way she kept on with the conversation, even when Jesus openly revealed his knowledge of her unacceptable lifestyle. Her question to those in the town to whom she related her experience is in the same vein. "Could he be the Messiah?" she asked them (John 4:29).

The last thing to notice is her courage. She was brave to keep up the conversation with Jesus at all. She was braver still to persevere with it even when she was taken steadily out of her depths! Bravest of all was her journey back into town to tell others about him, testimony which caused them to come and see him and believe. Their words to the woman may sound a little harsh. "We believe now, not because of what you said, but because we ourselves have heard him, and we know that he really is the Savior of the world" (John 4:42). Could it be that, even now, they would not bring themselves to give such a woman credit for her part in their spiritual pilgrimage? It seems quite clear that they would not have come to believe in Jesus themselves without her testimony. "Come and see the man who told me everything I have ever done" (John 4:29).

How did the woman at the well become a disciple? In her loneliness she met a person who had every reason to shun her and despise her. (He had more reason than she knew for doing so, since there were all the religious and moral reasons for ignoring her, but he knew about her private life too.) Instead of a man who might, as others had done, use her as an object of his sexual desires, she found instead a man who was willing to take her seriously as a person.

The second step in the process is Jesus' need that she might do something for him. John wishes us to know that his need for a drink was no pose. He says that Jesus, "tired out by the trip, sat down by the well. It was about noon" (John 4:6). But Jesus turned his physical need into an affirmation of an immoral Samaritan woman's worth. "Immoral," "Samaritan," "woman"— each is a reason for him to reject her. Instead he passes by all these obstacles and affirms her value as a person who can do something for him.

The third step is taken, however, when her reply, showing sensitivity to moral and religious issues, leads Jesus to ignore his own physical thirst for water, and he begins to point her toward the water of eternal life. Jesus' ability to use a material element as an image of spiritual reality opens the door to the Samaritan woman's salvation.

Jesus needs to do more than begin where she is and to point her in the right spiritual direction, however. Once she realizes how close he is getting to her own private life, she seeks to lead him off into historical and theological argument about which is the best place to worship God (John 4:19). He replies by pointing her straight back to the spiritual realities connected with God's gift of the Holy Spirit, enabling all who receive the Spirit to be free to worship God in spirit and in truth wherever they are (John 4:21-24). She is face to face with her own need for God again.

So the fifth step is taken. She talks of the future coming of the Messiah. He says, "I am he." Now she has to decide one way or the other. Her testimony to the townspeople, and its effects, suggests that her response was positive.

What theological insights are involved in the story of the woman at the well? First think what it means to see people "created in God's image," as Genesis 1 describes it. At very least it must have something to do with the ability to stand apart from a personal situation, reflect on it, reach a decision about it, act accordingly, and take the consequences. Although the presence of sin in human nature spoils this image, it does not destroy it altogether. It is like a beautiful building being spoiled, but not obliterated. One can still see signs of its former glory. So it is with sinful human nature, as careful observation makes clear.

This point was particularly important to John Wesley. Popular Calvinism in the eighteenth century involved belief about the total depravity of human beings, so that they were unable to respond to God's grace in Jesus. Wesley took the side of Arminius, who saw such teaching as an insult to God's creative work in human life. With the operation of prevenient grace in a person's life, it is possible for that person to respond to grace in a way which makes it his or her response. This was part of Wesley's reason for believing that in any crowd who heard the gospel message, each person was able to respond since God had made each one, and Christ had died for *all*. This is why so many of Charles Wesley's hymns contain reference to *all* people, such as "For all my Lord was crucified, for all, for all, my Savior died."

A person such as the woman at the well, who breaks a moral or cultural standard at one point, even flagrantly, is not thereby incapable of deep spiritual reflection, perception, and commitment. We too easily dismiss on those grounds the possibility of certain groups of people becoming Christians.

The second theological insight relates to incarnation as the clue to the importance of God's presence. Jesus lived among us in order to reach us. With this woman he began just exactly where she was. At a well he talked first about physical water, then about spiritual water. By beginning where she was, he provided the only possibility of leading her to where she needed to be. We should not underestimate the cost to Jesus in crossing the barriers to get to this point, or the antagonism created by this kind of action. The question is whether we care enough for people to take willingly such risks.

Much of the criticism of John Wesley arose precisely in terms of his determination to reach people with the Christian good news. When refused the pulpits in churches, he preached in graveyards and fields. Contrary to Church of England practice, he went into other clergymen's parishes and preached to those who were rarely, if ever, in church.

A third theological point arises from the way Jesus drew the woman's attention to her immoral life. In one sense the gospel is bad news before it is good news. She must face the fact that salvation is not about discussing moral, historical, and theological issues but about being forgiven and made clean by the spring of the inward presence of God's Holy Spirit. Not everyone begins the Christian life by being convicted of sin, but we do not progress far without facing it.

Whatever else Wesley's preaching lacked, it was not an emphasis on sin. His renowned (or infamous) sermon at St. Mary's Church, Oxford, which stunned the congregation into seething rage, was precisely about the human plight without conversion and new birth. This is why Charles Wesley's hymns also contain so much about sin and need for forgiveness. But it is freely available. Hence the offer of Jesus to the woman at the well.

What are we to learn from this woman's story about our mission? Place the content of the woman's story and this chapter into the context of our own lives, by asking particularly about the influence or moral standards in our culture, the lifestyles of men and women around us, and how in the light of this story, we can make the good news known to others.

1. How do moral standards in our *culture* determine whether or not you think a person is a Christian?

2. Are certain lifestyles totally unacceptable to the Christian community? Which ones? Do you each agree on which ones? Why are they unacceptable?

3. When you tell the good news to someone, or when someone tells it to you, should it include a strong rebuke if there is obvious sin present?

RITA

Rita was a nurse serving in the Middle East. She enjoyed the parties as well as the work and led a fairly loose moral life. In the course of this lifestyle she became involved not only with alcohol but with drugs, both against the law in the country where she worked. She was tried, found guilty, and imprisoned. She might have been condemned to death.

In prison she was visited regularly by a much older woman, a missionary who in Christ's name found Rita where she was in her loneliness and ministered to her there. Eventually Rita was able to admit her need for forgiveness through Christ.

When Rita was freed, she returned to Britain and became a clear and influential witness to Christ, the means of others becoming Christian through her testimony.

4
THE MAN BORN BLIND
John 9:1-41

This is a story about Jesus which stirs up strong emotions: sympathy for the man at the center of the story and anger toward almost everyone else. It also shows, in common with many of the Gospel stories, how much inner resource and perception are to be found in the most unlikely people.

Who was the man born blind? As before, we have only the essential information. Obviously, he was blind. We know from John 9:8 that he was a beggar, because this is what people said about him. "Isn't this the man who used to sit and beg?" He probably lived with his parents, since in John 9:18 we read that the authorities brought his parents for questioning about him. His mother and father seemed unwilling to take his side, however, and left it to him. That is the limit of our knowledge about his circumstances.

What kind of a person was the man born blind? The characteristics which stand out are his down-to-earth approach to life and his courage. After years of blindness he experiences a passer-by putting mud on his eyes and telling him to wash his face in the Pool at Siloam. He does so and receives his sight (John 9:6-8). John records no great excitement on his part, such as Luke describes in Acts 3 of the lame man who was healed at the Beautiful Gate of the Temple. By contrast this man simply returns to where he was, but he is now able to see. This probably explains partially why people could not believe that it was the same man (John 9:8-9). His matter-of-fact approach came out when they asked him what had happened. He simply recounted the events (John 9:11). When they asked him where Jesus was now, his answer could hardly have been briefer or less helpful. "I do not know" (John 9:12). He does not possess a gushing or excitable personality!

Lack of emotion did not mean lack of response, however. When the religious leaders question him about the alleged events, he again gives a short account (John 9:13-15). When asked what he has to say about the man who has healed him, however, he does have an answer, "He is a prophet" (John 9:17). When they make derogatory statements about Jesus, the healed man defends him, to the point of being expelled from the synagogue (John 9:24-34). His spirituality was down-to-earth in a very simple way. If God used a man to heal him, that man could not be the sinner some Pharisees were making him out to be. When, later, he learned more about Jesus, he became personally committed. Again, the words are brief, unfussy, and simple: "I believe, Lord!"

His courage is shown throughout the story. His neighbors will not even accept that he is the same person. His parents refuse to defend him because of threats of expulsion from the synagogue (John 9:22). Some Pharisees say that Jesus is a sinner, because he healed him on the Sabbath (John 9:16). In face of all this opposition, and on a basis of minimum knowledge, he resolutely sustains his loyalty to Jesus as a Prophet who has healed him. When he meets Jesus, and hears him speak of the Son of Man in personal terms, this same courage carries him on into wholehearted belief.

How did the man born blind become a disciple? In one sense the question is already answered. But the important elements in the story have not yet emerged. For example, this man, as far as we know, played no part in the process until Jesus came up to him and offered him healing. He was, in fact, though he probably did not know it, the subject of theological discussion between Jesus and his disciples. While the disciples saw in him nothing more than a theological problem ("Whose sin was it that caused him to be born blind?"), Jesus saw him as a person to be healed.

The first step toward his discipleship was not in the man's life at all. It was in Jesus' determination to turn a theological discussion into compassionate action. We are too often so dominated by the *how?* questions of the origin of things that we neglect to ask *why?* questions about what purpose can be achieved through them. The clue to the transition from *how?* to *why?* in this story, as so often, lay in stopping the theological discussion and getting on with powerful, compassionate action.

Second, although events overtook the blind man, he was not ignored. The man had not asked to be healed, but he was given the opportunity to show that he wished to be healed. Jesus could have healed him where he found him. Instead, having put mud on his eyes, he sent him to wash in the Pool at Siloam. His willingness to receive healing was an important part of the cure. He went and washed, and he could see.

A third important step was his ability to testify about what God had done for him. It is a gross understatement to say that he had much to learn! He was not properly a disciple of Jesus since he had not even properly met him. Yet what he knew, he resolutely defended in face of all opposition. He did not always get it right, as, for example, his claim (John 9:32), "Since the beginning of the world it has never been heard of that someone opened the eyes of a man born blind." Perhaps at this point he was claiming more than he could know! But in principle he had it right, and the more he witnessed to his own genuine experience, the stronger it became.

The crowning moment was the second time that Jesus found him. We exercise our imagination a little in picturing the man alone. After the frustrating experiences since his healing, he must have been feeling physically and nervously exhausted. When neighbors had rejected him, parents deserted him, and religious leaders attacked him, who was he to stand out alone? It would not be surprising if at that point he felt lonely and dispirited.

John says that Jesus discovered where he was and came to see him. To the man's experience of healing Jesus now added some theological and conceptual understanding. He asked him about the Son of Man. The response was quick and keen: "Tell me who he is, sir, so I can believe in him!" (John 9:36). The reply he received from Jesus was more surprising than his earlier experience of healing: "You have already seen him, and he is the one who is talking with you now" (John 9:37). As readily as he had gone to the Pool of Siloam for healing, he now affirms his faith. "I believe, Lord." John adds that he knelt down before Jesus (John 9:38).

What theological insights emerge from this story of the man born blind? The prevenience of grace is obvious. Grace reached him before he, being blind, was even aware of the proximity of Jesus, the center of divine grace. Grace literally found him.

Second, emphasis must be placed on the variety of the operation of grace. Christians often think of making disciples as an exercise in telling persons something to which they make response. In this case the gospel reached this man as compassionate action, the significance of which he only partly understood. There was something for him to respond to, but the response called for cooperative action, not intellectual assent to a statement. One wonders what would have happened if the first approach had been by words. He might not have been able either to comprehend or to respond. But a command to find the pool and wash for healing met his initial need perfectly.

Yet, third, to be the recipient of grace in action—grace dramatic enough to change his whole life, and grace effective enough for him to stand against the whole of society in its defense—was evidently not enough. He needed also to experience personal commitment to

Jesus as Son of God. Again, Jesus found him and led him to the faith. The conscious relationship with Christ lies at the heart of the discipleship.

Theologically and practically John Wesley found no difficulty in holding together compassionate action and evangelistic proclamation as part of the one gospel activity. Neither did he prescribe that one must precede or take preference over the other. To travel a quarter of a million miles by horse or carriage in the eighteenth century, and to preach over 40,000 times, reflects a strong commitment to proclamation! But the schools and orphanages, lending societies and healing work, popular publishing and class training, visiting of hospitals and prisons, all witness to Wesley's strong social conscience and program. Gospel peace and social justice belong inextricably together.

What lessons may we learn for discipleship from the man born blind? This story reveals yet another way in which a person became a disciple in Jesus' time. It is different from all the others looked at so far. It warns us against forcing people into molds, either in the way they become disciples of Jesus or in the ways in which they practice that discipleship. In particular here we need to reflect on how some people can only be reached by compassionate action to meet their need before they can respond to the gospel in words and explanations. Their initial responses may also be deeds, not words.

The story must also cause us to ask whether there are points at which we, like his neighbors because of unbelief, or his parents because of fear, or the Pharisees because of rigid opinions, refuse to recognize or are unable to recognize the grace of God already at work in other people's lives.

Where we are committed to social action, there is another question raised by British Bishop Lesslie Newbigin. All our Christian work is likely to have an element of missionary *dimension*. Anything we do as Christians raises in some form the question of why we do it. Bishop Newbigin asks, however, about our missionary *intention*. In all our social activities, do we intend that people should come to know, love, and serve Christ? We might apply the question to our evangelism too. Every bit of evangelistic activity will have some social *dimension*. We cannot invite people to be disciples of Christ without there being some social change in their lives. But is there any social *intention* in our evangelism? Do we really care about the circumstances of life enjoyed or endured by those to whom we preach and witness? Our honest answer to these questions will show how effectively or otherwise we hold together the two great areas of gospel activity, compassionate action or evangelistic proclamation.

1. Did you place your faith in Jesus Christ because of what someone did for or to you, or because of what he or she said to you?

2. In your attempt to be a good neighbor in your community, is the Christian message clear to those you serve? Describe the missionary *intention* in one particular service provided by the church in your community.

3. Have you ever been persecuted because of your Christian testimony or activity? If not personally, tell the story of someone you have heard about.

MARY

Mary was a permanently disabled woman. She was in a wheelchair for many years, cared for by her family and expecting to be so for the rest of her life.

One day, totally unexpectedly, she heard a voice in her head telling her to get up and walk! She took the voice at its word, tried to get out of the wheelchair, and found that she could do so! She got up and walked and has done so since.

She is convinced that the voice was the voice of God. She neither sought it nor expected it, but when it came she obeyed it, to her own great gain.

She has joined the Salvation Army in expression of the faith by which she now feels she must live.

5
MARY AND MARTHA
John 11:17-37

In turning to the story of Mary and Martha in John's Gospel we concentrate more on the art of *being* a disciple than on the ways of *becoming* one. It is not clear from the New Testament how and when they became disciples of Jesus, but their story tells us much about the quality of that discipleship, particularly in relation to the death of Lazarus, their brother.

Who were Mary and Martha? They were sisters. Their brother was Lazarus, and they often provided hospitality for Jesus and his followers. There was a deep love between Jesus and this family.

What kind of people were Mary and Martha? They were sisters, but they were different from one another. When Luke introduces them in his story he writes, "Jesus . . . came to a certain village where a woman named Martha welcomed him in her home. She had a sister named Mary" (Luke 10:38-39). The story goes on to tell how Mary sat listening to Jesus while Martha did all the work of caring for the guests. When Martha complained to Jesus—they must already have known him quite well—he replied "Martha, Martha! You are worried and troubled over so many things, but just one is needed. Mary has chosen the right thing, and it will not be taken away from her" (Luke 10:41-42). Lest we take this as too heavy a judgment for Mary and against Martha, notice that Luke tells this story straight after Jesus' parable of the Good Samaritan. In that story it is works of kindness which are not only praised but enjoined on the listeners. On the strength of that story it would be Martha and not Mary who scored well. Luke's point is not that one is better than the other but that they are different one from the other and that each has her honored place among Jesus' disciples.

John's Gospel identifies Mary as the woman who anointed Jesus' feet with perfume and wiped them with her hair (John 11:2). This adds poignancy to the warmth of Jesus' relationship to that whole family.

How are Mary and Martha being disciples? In this story of Lazarus' death the most startling fact is their implicit trust in the miraculous power of Jesus. When Lazarus became ill, they sent a message to Jesus, "Lord, your dear friend is sick" (John 11:3). For the very unexpected reason that it would all in the end work out for the glory of God, Jesus delayed two days before setting off for Bethany. He issued and received a rebuke from the sisters for delaying. He also received a rebuke from his disciples for going to Judaea at all (John 11:8). At times even Jesus could not please anybody!

The rebuke from the sisters is, however, gentle and full of faith. Each comes separately to Jesus, and each independently of the other uses the identical words, "If you had been here, Lord, my brother would not have died!" (John 11:21, 32). With different personalities, and experiences, they find complete unanimity in their loyalty to and faith in Jesus.

Apart from that, their responses are different again. Martha, perhaps more in control of herself and the situation, is the first to be told of Jesus' arrival. Was it common knowledge that Martha was the one better able to receive such news? When she has addressed her "rebuke of faith" to Jesus, a significant theological discussion unfolds (John 11:22-27), introduced by a comment from Martha. When Mary arrives to see Jesus, having been told of his presence by

Martha, perhaps as things usually happened, the result is very different. Mary blurts out thoughts and then dissolves into tears (John 11:32-33). There was no chance for theological discussion or any other kind of discussion. She was simply too upset.

Yet John's use of this story is deeply moving. Martha's discussion with Jesus enables him to lead her to a declaration of faith which really provides the setting for Lazarus to be raised. She says that even now God would enable Jesus to perform a miracle for Lazarus. Jesus says, "Your brother will rise to life." Martha, not daring to hope too much, affirms the resurrection on the last day. Jesus claims that he is the resurrection and the life, and that no one who believes in him will die. She affirms this, "Yes, Lord! . . . I do believe that you are the Messiah, the Son of God, who was to come into the world" (John 11:21-27). A framework of faith is now in place which can give meaning to the raising of Lazarus, meaning in relation to Lazarus, and meaning in relation to Jesus.

Mary does not appear capable of such a discussion, or such an affirmation. Yet since she is the woman who anointed the feet of Jesus with perfume and dried them with her hair, then maybe she has already said this and more, by these eloquent, extravagant actions; things which she cannot put into words. If so, she may perceive these things intuitively before Martha does!

In this story, however, her contribution is different. Martha gives will and mind: Mary gives emotion. Indeed John daringly suggests that her weeping, and that of the other mourners, finally touches Jesus so deeply that he moves on to see the tomb and raise Lazarus from it.

It is as though John wants us to see that alone neither of the sisters is capable of the whole response Jesus looked for, but that together they do so. Different in personality and experience, different in roles at home and in the fellowship, together they bring a wholeness which otherwise eluded both of them. Neither could be the other; each needs the other. Jesus needs them both. So does Lazarus.

What theology lies beneath this story? The body of Christ is one of the major pictures of the church in the New Testament. Paul uses this image powerfully to show how each part of the body needs all the other parts, and how each should be honored, even though their importance varies. The church of Jesus Christ needs desperately to learn and apply this lesson today. There are at least four separate and legitimate reasons why the church is made up of individuals and groups who understand and practice their Christianity in different ways. One reason is that God is far beyond our ability to comprehend. He is by definition different from his creatures. We perceive dimly what he reveals of himself to us. None of us can grasp it all. It is therefore likely that others of us will have insights into particular facets of God's being, and that we must hold those insights for the sake of the rest.

A second reason for our differences from one another is that our contexts are different. Our perception of life is colored by our heredity, environment, abilities, and experience. Out of that particular blend we are fitted or unfitted to be aware of parts of God's being. It is not surprising, for example, that "liberation theology" flourishes among oppressed peoples in South America and among black Christians in the United States of America. They need to hold these views on behalf of the whole Christian family, too.

A third reason for divergence of belief and practice is that we differ from one another in basic personality. Since God finds us where we are and leads us to himself from there, it is not surprising that who we are should have significant influence on our understanding and activity as Christians.

Fourth, God gives different gifts to his people, and the gifts we receive color our way of describing and living the Christian life. Personal preferences for evangelism, social care, struggle for justice, nurturing the life of the church are all intimately related to this and the previous point. As one Christian discussion group concluded, the unity of the Christian church will always be like the unity of a bunch of varied flowers.

Yet Mary and Martha add one absolutely crucial point to these reflections. Although these sisters seem to have been so different in personality and experience, John portrays them as being absolutely at one in the conviction that Jesus could have saved Lazarus' life had he been there. Our common conviction about Jesus Christ, and our common allegiance to God through him, are fundamental to the oneness of the church, which is his Body. We need ways, and we need the will and patience, to put into practice the ancient guideline, "In essentials, unity; in differences, humility; in all things, love."

Wesley's sermon on "The Catholic Spirit" provides a model for such an approach. He makes it clear that his first question to another person is not about doctrine ("opinions," as he put it in eighteenth century terms), ethics, or churchmanship. The crucial question is, based on 2 Kings 10:15, "Is your heart right, as my heart is with yours?" That is, do we have a common allegiance to God in Christ? "If so then," continues Wesley, quoting Jehu from his text, "give me your hand."

This is not to minimize the importance of seeking truth in belief and practice. Quite the opposite. In spite of his sermon on the catholic spirit, Wesley still had some very critical things to say about Christians whom he judged to be wrong in doctrine or practice. Once we have established a uniting personal commitment to God in Christ, and have taken one another's hand, then the real task begins of exploring together what we believe about doctrine, ethics, church hierarchy, and a host of other issues. The genuineness of our commitment to Christ is reflected in the seriousness of our search for truth in these matters. But it becomes a search together, by members of the one family; not a battlefield from artificially constructed trenches. The nearer we are to Christ as the center, the nearer we shall be to one another.

What can we learn from this story of Mary and Martha?

The closeness of Mary and Martha as sisters makes the differences between them all the more striking. The differences between them in character and experience make their oneness about Jesus all the more moving. We do well to reflect on the significance of that for our relationship with other Christians and other groups of Christians, and about its importance for our understanding of how to lead others to discipleship out of the great variety of human personality and experience.

1. Mary and Martha had two different ways of trusting Jesus. What were these approaches? Which one best fits your personality?

2. Describe how your personal context for being a Christian disciple is different from a close relative (such as a spouse or sibling) or a good friend. Explain yourself in terms of heredity, environment, and ability.

3. Invite to one of your Christian study groups a speaker from another denomination (e.g., Catholic or other Protestant body). Have this speaker explain how you agree and differ in your Christian beliefs and commitments.

TOM AND JOAN

Joan and Tom have a traditional marriage. Their marriage is actually rare in today's world because the roles of the husband and wife can easily be reversed. He is a highly trained government official. She is a housewife who has not worked for income since they were married.

Tom is highly articulate, deeply thoughtful, well read, and sensitive to current issues. He is trained to turn problems inside out, to assemble available evidence and sift it, to look as objectively as possible and reach a balanced view. Joan is warm, welcoming, good at relationships, and runs an efficient home. She does not speak in public gatherings or lead meetings. They appear to be complementary persons at almost every point in their married life together.

One place of total sameness is their commitment to Christ, their loyalty within The Methodist Church, their worship, and their devotional life. However, in their search for truth, their journeys are very different. He thinks, reads, wrestles, reflects, discusses, and concludes. She feels her way there intuitively, and is often there ahead of him. Her commitment is no less, nor is her discipleship less effective. Their relationship is a living testimony to the variety of ways of becoming and remaining a disciple of Jesus. They are an example of the wider diversity of the church.

6
THOMAS
John 20:24-29

Thomas may well have been the most difficult to get along with of all the disciples! John's Gospel includes a number of references to him, each of them suggesting unusual characteristics by contrast with the other disciples. We know he was a disciple. We know he was called "the Twin," and we know that because of the passage we are now to study he is widely described as "doubting Thomas." We infer that this was not a good thing to be.

What kind of person was he? There are glimpses in the Gospels. In John's account he appears four times. In the last of these, John 21:2, he is listed with other disciples who were together after some of the resurrection appearances of Jesus. In common with the other disciples, Thomas agrees to go fishing with Peter. There is nothing distinctive about that. The other three references to Thomas, however, are different.

First, in John 11:16, Jesus had received from Martha and Mary the story that Lazarus their brother, for whom Jesus had deep affection, was very ill. Unpredictably Jesus did not rush at once, but stayed two further days (John 11:1-6). The delay suited the disciples fine, since they knew that Judaea meant danger (John 11:8). But Jesus announced that they would now go back (John 11:7). This introduces discussion about doing what is right, and about whether or not Lazarus will recover. Jesus tells them openly that Lazarus is dead but that they must go to him. It is here that two of Thomas' characteristics emerge—wisdom to perceive the true nature of a situation and courage to tell it even if the news is not good.

"Let us all go along with the Teacher," says Thomas "so that we may die with him!" He was evidently what we would describe today as a realist. For all the discussion about Lazarus, Thomas knew that to go to Judaea was to court disaster. He was bold enough to say it (forcing others to face a reality they may have wished to avoid), and to suggest that they all nevertheless go with Jesus and die with him (maybe forcing others into action which they would also have wished to avoid).

In John 14:5 Thomas appears again. This time is also the occasion of Jesus shocking his disciples by something he taught. He tells them that he will be leaving them (John 13:33). In his absence they are to love one another as a witness to the world (John 13:34-35). Simon Peter (of course!) asked the first question, "Where are you going, Lord?" (John 13:36). Jesus' answer led to the affirmation by Jesus, "You know how to get to the place where I am going," (John 14:4). We must try to enter imaginatively into the mood of that occasion. There was shock at the thought of Jesus leaving, when they knew how much work remained to be done. There would also be an almost desperate desire to accept whatever Jesus told them, as a source of security.

It was not so for Thomas. He did not understand, and he said so, in terms that are almost reproachful. "Lord, we do not know where you are going; how can we know the way to get there?" (John 14:5). Thomas is presented as a man not easily influenced by a strong group feeling unless it is to resist it. Whatever the corporate mood of the moment was, there were things Thomas did not understand. Indeed, as far as he was concerned, what Jesus had said about knowing the way was not even true. Their shocked condition might lead them to pretend they understood when they did not. Thomas would not allow that to happen. Their reverence for Jesus, and their deep desire not to lose him, might cause them to acquiesce in statements they did not believe to be true. Thomas would not allow that either. There was evidence he lacked. He must have it. Ignorance was being passed over. He must declare it. An inaccurate statement had been made. He must correct it.

It may be that the other disciples did not approve of Thomas speaking in that blunt way. It may have seemed to them as though he were spoiling a profoundly deep moment with his sharp statement. It may even be that some were shocked by his apparent rebuke to Jesus in saying what Thomas denies to be true. They do not know the way. On the other hand, some may have been glad that Thomas made such a statement. Perhaps they often relied on him to ask the questions they dared not ask, or to make the statement they would hesitate to make. Whatever the psychological mood of the disciples may have been, Thomas' words gave rise to one of the most profound statements ever ascribed to Jesus: "I am the way, the truth, and the life; no one goes to the Father except by me. Now that you have known me . . . you will know my Father also; and from now on you do know him, and you have seen him" (John 14:6-7). Thomas' realistic question gave rise to Jesus' self-revelation. His searching led to that discovery, and even if it does not seem yet to have been true in Thomas' experience, the words of Jesus have combined profundity and simplicity in lifting them to a level of understanding of him hitherto impossible. But it took a stubborn questioner to make it possible for the whole group.

How did Thomas become a disciple? It is in the light of these two passages that we approach John 20:24-29. Here we have a situation which separated Thomas from the other disciples even more strikingly. John tells us (John 20:24) that Thomas missed the late Sunday evening appearance of Jesus, described in John 20:19-23. They had heard him give them his peace. He had sent them out as his Father had sent him. He had breathed on them as a sign of their receiving the Holy Spirit. He had even encouraged them to preach the gospel in a way which forgave or did not forgive the sins of others. Their excitement and enthusiasm must have been very great indeed.

We may ask, in passing, why Thomas was not with them on that Sunday evening. Was he simply braver than the rest, since John says they were behind locked doors through fear of the Jewish authorities (John 20:19)? Or were doubts getting stronger in Thomas' mind? Had he more and more questions unanswered? John's description in 20:24 does seem to go out of its way to make the point of his absence. "Thomas called the Twin" would have been adequate as a description. But John describes him as "Thomas, *one of the twelve disciples* (called the Twin)." Is John drawing attention to Thomas' negligence in not being there?

Whatever the reason, it is clear that the others found Thomas and, in a mood of high excitement, told him, "We saw the Lord!" (John 20:25). Now some of his characteristics emerge. He will not accept something just because they say so. His first response to their confident claim to have seen the Lord was, "If I do not see . . . I will not believe." He would only join the ranks of the believers in the risen Lord if he could see for himself. It must be personal to him and convincing for him. Their experience could not stand in for his.

The other remarkable element in Thomas' response concerns the type of evidence he required. Human beings use all kinds of characteristics by which to recognize other human beings— appearance, voice, walk, and so on. Thomas focuses on the nail marks in the hands of Jesus and the spear mark in his side, wounds from the crucifixion of Jesus. Only that evidence would convince him that whomever or whatever he might see in the future truly was Jesus, the Lord.

We may feel that Thomas was wrong to ask for proof of this kind. Who was he to make such demands? Yet the others had received such a privilege. At least he seemed to believe he also might see the risen Christ. And we can surely only commend his determination to experience the risen Lord for himself; his resistance of the temptation to pretend to believe because they did, or even to allow their confidence to carry him along. He was right to want to know for himself, to have this fundamental question answered.

The Gospel of John says Thomas got what he wanted. Or did he? John 20:26-29 tells how one week later, on the first day of the week, resurrection day, Jesus appeared again to the disciples, and that this time Thomas was there. Jesus singled him out, offered him the evidence he had requested, the wounds in hands and side. There was also an injunction, "Stop your doubting, and believe!" So Thomas did get what he wanted. And yet, oddly enough, he did not take it. For the story to develop naturally we would have expected Thomas to stretch out a finger and touch the wound in the hand, and to feel with his own hand the scars in Jesus' side. But he did not do so. In fact he simply replied, "My Lord and my God!"

Why does the story take this turn? Is it not out of keeping with the portrait of Thomas in John's Gospel? In response to the claims of the others, Thomas rightly insisted that any faith must be his own. In face of the unasked question, "What evidence would satisfy you?", Thomas stipulates evidence directly relevant to their latest knowledge of Jesus, and most contradictory of their claims that he was alive; namely that he was crucified, and so dead. What had now happened to him, however, put the whole question of spiritual reality into different perspective. He was experiencing the presence of the risen Christ. Why would he need to confirm the details of hand and side wounds when he had now moved onto a different level of awareness altogether? Talk of detailed proof became irrelevant in the comprehensive presence of the risen Christ who had conquered death and sin. He was being invited to reach, by faith, whole areas of reality not accessible to proof. This is why Jesus said to him, "Do you believe because you see me? How happy are those who believe without seeing me!" The Lord was not talking about gullibility; Jesus was talking about faith as the only way to find knowledge in some areas of life, in the way that proof is the only way to find knowledge in others.

What theological issues are raised by this story? First, there is the emphasis upon evidence in relation to Christian believing. Thomas must have been an uncomfortable companion to have, but he is presented as one who wanted to go to the facts and to face them, whenever possible. His refusal to be quiet when he was ignorant of the facts in John 14 led to one of our Lord's most profound statements about himself. His insistence on seeing for himself what he considered convincing evidence, before he would believe, protected him from being carried along by the exciting experience of others. He did not, in the end, need the detailed evidence he had demanded. But he did receive a personal revelation of the risen Christ, which was necessary for him.

Christianity is not opposed to reason or the use of the mind. One has only to look at Paul's references to the mind in the letter to the Romans to see the importance of reason. Reason cannot operate on the basis of proof in a scientific sense, since it is about faith. Yet faith is not a blind leap in the dark. It is a commitment of oneself to a person, a message, and a way of life on a basis of evidence which encourages such a commitment. In that whole process the mind must be wholly involved if faith is to be realistic.

Nevertheless, Thomas was to learn a second theological lesson in his experience of the risen Lord. To believe "only according to what I see physically" is to limit one's perception enormously. When he had the chance to touch the wounds of Jesus, he did not take it. In perceiving the presence of the risen Jesus he realized that he had moved into a different, though related, world of reality altogether. And the words of Jesus to him, "How happy are those who believe without seeing me," suggest that for most believers in the future there will be a form of spiritual perception which does not even require the sight of the risen Christ. They will begin further down the line of believing than Thomas did. For them, becoming a disciple will also relate to evidence, but it will be the evidence of Christ in the lives of others, of the news of Jesus in the Scriptures, and of perception of his work in their own lives. They will begin by "seeing" in the sense of spiritually perceiving the risen Christ, not in the sense of physically observing him. Thomas still had that kind of lesson to learn. Yet the seeking evidence/perceiving/believing process is the same for both.

Both the search for evidence and the awareness of its limited capacity where spiritual matters are concerned, are important for understanding what it means to be a disciple. When Isaac Watts wrote:

> Where reason fails, with all its powers;
> Then faith prevails, and love adores

we must notice that he does speak of "all reason's powers," though limited. Faith and love go further then reason, but they neither abandon it nor disqualify it.

Another theological point emerges. "The faith" in the sense both of the act of believing and the content of what is believed, can be defended. There is a fundamental "reasonableness" about it which can be described and affirmed. This process is sometimes called Apologetics, defending the faith reasonably and intellectually. Unless the church as a whole fulfills that task, she makes her evangelistic work all the harder. But to do so with integrity, the church must ensure that her worship and teaching, her thinking and speaking, do take seriously the importance of the mind in the faith of the believer.

John Wesley took this point with severe seriousness, warning that the person who departed from reason would very soon depart from religion altogether. He was certainly, as he described himself, "a man of one book" (the Bible), but he also read, and wrote, many others. His reading list for his preachers is awe-inspiring! The bibliography provided for the children of his Kingswood School makes one wonder how anyone ever had the courage to begin or the perseverance to end the course! Wesley produced large numbers of small booklets, small enough to be carried, cheap enough to be afforded, short enough to be read by ordinary people. He patiently, at length, and rationally answered criticisms and questions. His published sermons are models of sane and logical thought. Methodists who are true to their heritage will neither go against reason nor neglect serious thought.

Yet Wesley went beyond reason. He recognized and affirmed the miraculous in Christian experience. His teaching on assurance and scriptural holiness involves whole areas of experience beyond the powers of human reason to explain, though human reason was valuable in describing them. There is not a conflict between reason and faith except where people try to make either of them do the work of both.

What can we learn about discipleship from Thomas' story? First, spiritual development must never seek to bypass the mind. Second, to ask deep and searching questions is not a sign of unbelief. Third, therefore, in trying to help others into faith we may need patiently to answer very many questions. Fourth, however, if we are to enter into discipleship, or to grow in it, there must also be willingness to take steps of faith on the basis of evidence provided in order to experience areas of reality not susceptible to reason. The interaction between reason and faith, information and commitment, knowledge and perception varies greatly between one person and another. We need patience to help one another and humility to learn from one another in this crucial part of our service to God.

1. Can you think of a person who fills the role of Thomas in the life of the church? What is his or her contribution?

2. How can we ensure that the mind plays a full enough part in our Christian experience individually and as a church?

3. How would you describe the place of reason and faith in your Christian experience?

SAL

The world of popular music attracts many of our young people. Russian groups are now becoming famous, and a recent riot in East Berlin was caused by the desire of large numbers of young people to hear a British "pop" group playing on the West Berlin side of the wall.

Sal is a singer in that world. Nominally a Roman Catholic, he enjoyed all the pleasures that go with being a music star if the star wants them. Yet having gone through one experience after another, posing one question after another to the way of life his religious beginnings would require, he still found himself unsatisfied.

One day, in the quietness of a convent garden during a visit to Europe, he suddenly knew with deep certainty where real satisfaction lies. He was convinced of the reality of God and of the need to serve Jesus Christ.

He continues on as a "pop" star, but much of his spare time is given to reaching young people, especially disadvantaged young people, to show something of God's love to them.

7
THE PARALYTIC
Mark 2:1-12

In Mark's Gospel the concentration often tends to be more on the action than on the people involved. His main concern is to portray Jesus, in the early part of his account, as the strong miracle worker. We do better with this story (and those that follow in Part Two) to watch the unfolding of the Gospel account, without losing sight of the man who was healed.

There was a crowd to whom Jesus was preaching the good news of the kingdom. This setting provided both the focal point and the context for what was to happen. It was in an atmosphere of the preaching and the receiving of the Word of God that the miracle from God was performed and experienced.

What do we know about the paralytic? The paralyzed man plainly wished to be cured. Otherwise he would not have submitted to the difficulties involved, which were not without their danger, in being brought to Jesus. He must have believed that Jesus could cure him. He had friends who believed it, too (Mark 2:5, "Jesus saw how much faith *they* had").

How did God's grace reach the paralytic? In the context as described, there was no way this man could have got to Jesus. Jesus responded to the interruption as the man was lowered down in front of him. Although his prime commitment was to proclaim the kingdom, it is also true that again and again there was a focusing of the kingdom on the needs of individuals. So now he stops his preaching to heal the paralytic in front of him.

Jesus' reaction caused offense. He told the man that his sins were forgiven. The religious leaders present were shocked by this, since they knew that only God could forgive sins in this way. Mark is firmly declaring the fact that if this man is forgiven, then that is an act of God, performed by Jesus.

Jesus puts two possible lines of action before his critics. Is it harder to offer forgiveness of sins or healing of the body? The answer is obvious. If you offer forgiveness, no one will know whether or not anything has been achieved. If you offer healing to a paralyzed man, however, it will be plain for all to see whether he is healed or not. He will move and walk, or he will remain immobile.

What happened next in the story is both puzzling and liberating. It is puzzling because Jesus says that in order to prove that he can do that one thing he is going to do the other! It is liberating, because once a person grasps how two important elements of gospel work are being brought together, new insights are possible.

Jesus says that to prove he can forgive sins he will heal the man's paralysis. He then proceeds to do so. At the practical level he performs the outward miracle that can be observed (the "harder" thing) to demonstrate that the inner miracle (the "easier" thing) has also been performed. The healing is the "marker" for the forgiveness.

Did the paralytic receive more than he expected? He had a deep physical need of which he was only too painfully aware. We do not know whether or not he was equally aware of an inner spiritual need. If he had much knowledge of the teaching being given by Jesus, he must have known that the emphasis was on inner healing. But the primary concern must have been physical restoration. His friends brought him into a context of faith and healing, and their (and his) faith was rewarded. The man was healed, inwardly and outwardly.

What theological ideas emerge through this story of the paralytic? First there is an insight from the biblical doctrine of creation: how much we need each other. The early chapters of Genesis have been interpreted so consistently in terms of our dependence upon and duty toward God that we have neglected another vital strand in those chapters. Human beings are also dependent upon and have a duty toward one another. Adam and Eve, Cain and Abel, Abram and Lot—story after story makes the same point. It is not that we *have the opportunity* to help others, or that we *have the privilege* to be helped by others, though both of these are true. It is that life is meant to have at its heart this mutual dependence. Failure to help someone in need is not just unworthy, it is a blow struck at the nerve center of human life. This is why loving one's neighbor is second only to loving God in the teaching of both Old and New Testaments. It is also why evangelism should be motivated primarily by love of those who do not know Christ. It is why fellowship—sharing with one another—is a fundamental activity within the Christian church. The men who carried their friend to Jesus were acting in harmony with the biblical understanding of creation and redemption.

A second theological lesson, all the more significant because it is placed by Mark so early in his Gospel, concerns the status of Jesus. The statement by the teachers of the law that God is the only one who can forgive sins (Mark 2:7), sets the scene for Jesus to forgive the man's sins. Mark's message is clear. Jesus is seen to do what only God can do. What does that tell us about Jesus?

The third theological implication concerns the linking, by Jesus, of the healing and the forgiving. The healing is not just a marker, it is a sign. We do not have to see the man's illness as a direct result of his sins, though this undoubtedly does happen in human experience. It is rather that Jesus is declaring that all the parts of a person's life belong together and, more important, that he has come to bring them together in a harmony which depends on a proper relationship to God. As one writer put it, the healing of the paralytic is not just *joined* to the forgiveness of the paralytic; it is a *sacrament* of that forgiveness. Jesus was not just making him well: He was making him *whole*.

Our separation of spirit and body does not help us to understand biblical teaching, which holds them together in a unity. To separate them opens up the possibility of seeing concern for people's souls and concern for their bodies as options; or of treating evangelism and socio-political action as alternatives for the church. This story underlines the fact that God sees us and loves us as total human beings, and that he expects us to have that attitude toward one another.

Our Methodist heritage illustrates these points well, though the popular view of the eighteenth century religious movement is often defective. The evangelism and the preaching are well known. What is less familiar is the concern to do something for those in asylums, to visit the prisoner, provide education for poor children, orphanages for the abandoned, physical healing for the neglected. John Wesley twice protested to the authorities about the treatment of French prisoners of war at Knowle, near Bristol. Toward the end of his life he was out in the snow-covered streets of London, collecting for the poor. His last letter was to William Wilberforce, encouraging him in his fight against the slave trade.

For the high view of the nature of Jesus in this passage we turn to the hymns of Charles Wesley. What can compare with the lovely Christmas lines:

> God the invisible appears:
> God the blest, the great I AM,
> Sojourn in the vale of tears,
> And Jesus is his name.
>
> Emptied of His majesty,
> Of His dazzling glories shorn,
> Being's source begins to be,
> And God himself is born.

The third theological lesson, the linking of soul and body, is reflected in Wesley's teaching on Perfect Love. Certainly there are theological and philosophical difficulties with the doctrine. Yet at heart it is about God's perfect love so dominating the sources of our being that whatever we think, say, or do springs from love. People so influenced may not always get it right, but the well from which they draw is right, because it is love. There is no room here for dividing the disciple, nor those he or she is concerned about, into souls and bodies. The unity of love underlies the wholeness of people.

What can we learn from this story of the paralytic? First the context of preaching and receiving the gospel must be the setting for healing to take place. We might ask whether our church, congregation, fellowship, or society provides such a context. Within the family of a believing community many people are made inwardly whole, even when their physical disablements are not removed. Equally, many are physically fit, but some are spiritually unwell.

Second, some people need other people to help them to the place where they can find wholeness. Christians too easily imagine that if we set up a place of worship and fellowship, then others should come. Yet Jesus himself was constantly meeting people where they were. He sent his disciples out to perform their mission. If we will not go where they are, they may never find their way to where *we* are.

Third, evangelism involves ministering to the needs of the whole person. We are not free to offer one part of the gospel ministry as though it were the whole. The offer of inner forgiveness and peace, the ministry of social and physical caring, and the struggle to bring justice for the poor all belong together. We may not be able to do them all at the same time. The circumstances in which we find people may require us to begin with one or other of the component parts. Yet we must never forget that they belong together and that we have not finished our work in anyone's life till this wholeness is complete. Since each of us is likely to be gifted and predisposed to move down one or other of these areas of ministry, it follows that we need one another very much if our task is to be completed.

1. Does your congregation provide a gospel context for healing in your community? Give one example.

2. Healing is a sign or marker of the gospel. Give two other actions which are markers of the gospel.

3. Some churches more than others put great emphasis on divine physical healing. In light of the paralytic's story, what is your view on the subject?

BILLIE

Billie was an Irish Protestant whose father was killed in 1970 by members of the I.R.A. He himself joined an illegal para-military force in Belfast, called the Ulster Volunteer Force (U.V.F.). Under their orders he killed a Protestant believed to be an informer.

At first, in prison he felt proud to be there. Then disillusionment set in and he thought of what he had done to someone else's family—exactly the same as had been done to his. Four happenings led to a dramatic change in his life. First he received (and he still does not know how) religious literature from New Zealand. He had no interest in it, so passed it on to another prisoner whom he knew to be a

Christian, and for whom he had little respect, regarding him as a softie who needed a crutch to keep him up. Billie did not need such support. Then the U.V.F. decided on a protest in prison. Billie decided against taking part, but on being told his legs would be broken he agreed to participate. He noticed that the Christian he had despised did not take part, and managed always to be bright and friendly despite all the pressures. Third, a prison officer, seeing Billie looking at the Christian man, said to Billie, "The difference between you and him is that he has Christ, and that is your need too." Fourth, an older woman kept on visiting him in an official capacity and presented her witness to him.

On Christmas Eve 1983 the aged woman read to him the story from Luke 23 of the dying thief on the Cross who called on Jesus for help. She advised Billie to think seriously about his life, about his need, and about God's love for him in Jesus. Billie did so.

Quite suddenly, in prison, Billie found himself face-to-face with God's challenge. He felt deeply convicted of the sin of murder, and realized that Jesus had died for him in love so that he might be forgiven. He gave his life there and then. Next day, of course, there were doubts, but the woman visited him and pointed him to John 6:37, where Jesus says, "I will never turn away anyone who comes to me."

He had much mockery and criticism to put up with in prison. His sentence was not shortened at all. He grew in his faith and is now, after release, studying to become a Baptist minister. When, on television, he was faced with some deep theological questions which he (and probably no one else) could answer, he replied, "One thing I do know. God laid his hand on my life in prison and changed me completely."

8
THE WOMAN WITH THE
HEMORRHAGE
Mark 5:25-34

Another of Mark's stories emphasizes the power of Jesus. In this story, however, there are several unusual developments. There is also a stronger concentration on the person with whom Jesus is dealing. The setting is different from that in Mark 2 and the story of the paralytic. A common feature is the crowd, but here it is a moving crowd. Jesus is not speaking to people in a formal way. He is walking with an interested crowd jostling around him. For one person this situation is ideal.

What do we know about the woman in this story? She was a sick woman because of a chronic bleeding complaint. Some things about her are very clear. She had done all she could to get well by spending money on doctors. Instead she was worse. (Luke, the physician, in his Gospel simply says that she wasn't any better!)

Second, she had heard about Jesus. Someone had no doubt told her that he healed people. She believed it.

Point three shows even more clearly what kind of woman she was. On the one side she had very large faith. "If I just touch his clothes I will get well," she told herself. She had no difficulty in believing that the power exerted through Jesus could heal her. But she wanted neither publicity nor fuss. She was going for a way which avoided any personal meeting with Jesus. No talk, no face-to-face meeting, no questions, and no answers. Just one touch of his clothes and she would be well. After all, the power was there.

How did she become a disciple of Jesus? Mark simply

tells us that she was right on every count in her assessment of the way to be cured. "She touched his cloak, and her bleeding stopped at once; and she had the feeling inside herself that she was healed of her trouble." We may be inclined, in these more scientific days, to want to stop to discuss the likelihood of such a cure, but Mark is in a hurry to draw our attention to two much more significant parts of the story.

The first is that the power that healed her came through Jesus, and he knew it. Mark says that, to the amazement of his followers, Jesus felt that power had gone from him, and therefore asked who touched him. His disciples could hardly believe that their master would ask such a question, with so many people pressing around him. But he wanted to know who had benefitted from his power. It is neither a matter of magic nor of manipulating certain systems. Divine power through Jesus was transmitted through personal relationship. Both Jesus' disciples and the woman involved needed to know that. We do well not to forget it, either. It is not the manifestation of divine power which is most important: it is the loving relationship it either establishes or enhances. That is one reason why Jesus refused to perform miracles either to show his power or to compel faith. It is also why he didn't refuse healing to anyone who needed it.

There is a second reason why Mark rushes us on: Jesus had more personal insight for the woman. Mark wishes us to know that the woman herself had not yet received all that Jesus had for her. She had experienced his power. Alone that would not save her. Covered in confusion, therefore, she makes her way to him in response to his question about who had touched him. Mark says that "she came, trembling with fear, fell at his feet, and told him the whole truth." The purposes of the kingdom had not been met by her method of touching and running. Those purposes are deeply personal and involve open relationship with God through Jesus. When she told him the whole truth, Jesus made clear what had now happened. Her faith was the vehicle of her healing. She had experienced power. More important still, he now sent her away at peace.

What theology emerges through this story? There is first a highlighting of human need in our approach to God through Jesus. This woman knew of her physical need. Even though Jesus met that need, he perceived that she had other needs too. She came to receive an injection of divine power; she went away with inward peace. Her perception of her need brought her there. Jesus' perception of her need made her totally well.

Part of our difficulty in dealing with need in relation to conversion has been the relentless emphasis on "conviction of sin" as the only acceptable evidence of a sense of need. Countless Christian testimonies show, however, that many do not begin on the road of Christian discipleship with a sense of sin. For many that comes later. Yet those who begin without a sense of sin still have a need for God, and often a felt need for God. Some need the answers to intellectual enquiry. Some need physical cure. Some need to feel loved, or to feel that they matter to someone. Some need assurance that life has a purpose.

This story in Mark 5 responds to such issues in two ways. It assures us that whatever the need, faith in Jesus will put us in touch with a power that makes a difference to our situation. Second, it informs us that whatever need brings us to Jesus, we are likely to discover other, possibly deeper, needs in our lives which Jesus wishes to address as we become aware of them.

John Wesley's doctrine of Christian Perfection is significant at this point. Over against a Roman Catholic system which provided for a variety of ways of making amends for inevitable sins, and a Calvinistic system which so devalued human capacity as to expect constant failures, Wesley taught optimism of grace which set no limits to what God can do in human lives which are open to the fullness of his love. One or other need, failure, weakness, or habit might be the reason for our turning to God in the first place, but divine love could deal with every one of them.

The second theological element in the story is the importance of simple faith. One wonders which counsel this woman would have received had she asked advice from the teachers of the law, or even the disciples of Jesus! In her own very simple—we might even think misguided—way she believed she could touch the clothing of Jesus and be healed. We deal with mystery here, since no one knows what actually happened. Mark does want us to understand that she did not heal herself by her act of faith. The section of the story where Jesus shows awareness of power going from him is given prominence. All we can say is that her simple faith somehow put her in touch with divine power in a way which led to healing. Of course the presence of Jesus, and the ministry he conducted, inspired the faith she showed, and so we could go on. The theological point seems to be that divine power is operative in the world and that the simplest form of faith can put us in touch with it. We need to guard against superstition on one side and our sophistication on the other side. We can be too simple or too clever. But in between these two poles there is a broad range of responses in faith through which God has chosen to work.

John Wesley had to learn this lesson again and again as the Methodist movement grew. Even to preach in the open air ("field preaching," as it was called) was difficult for him to accept. People converted outside the church walls seemed improper to him. He had problems, too, with the excited reaction some of his preaching provoked, with people shouting out and falling down under conviction of sin. He did not like the idea of lay people becoming preachers, as his correspondence with his mother over the case of Thomas Maxfield shows. Initially he distrusted activities like love-feasts and watchnight services lest they led to abuse. Yet again and again he discovered that the simple faith of ordinary people was an avenue of divine power.

The third theological issue is a necessary complement to the second. The woman had to discover that salvation is not just about receiving power in some impersonal way. It is also about a personal relationship with the divine healer. Salvation is about being open with God in Christ about ourselves. It is essentially a personal experience in which we learn not to hide things from him because we cannot achieve it anyway. As she told him all, she received his word of peace. In the Bible, peace is not simply the absence of war. It is a state of well-being based on the conviction that God has us in his care.

Openness about ourselves, as the way to inner peace, was a significant part of the early Methodist fellowship. John Wesley commended the practice of speaking "plain and home"; that is, frankly and bluntly. The Methodist meetings—whether for business, as at the annual conference, or for fellowship, as in the bands and classes—faced a set of questions which had to be answered. The custom continues on the business side to this day in various parts of Methodism. Questions about faithfulness to the doctrine, administering the discipline, overcoming temptation, or falling into sin, were all ways of enabling the Methodist people to "live out in the open" before God, as the woman in this story of Mark's was obliged to do. The degree of commitment to this principle in Wesley's day is shown by the final question for the band meetings. Having confessed their failures and shared their success, they faced a final question asking if there was anything in their lives about which they were not sure whether it was a sin! No fudging of spiritual issues was allowed. Like the woman in Mark 5, they were required to tell "the whole truth" (Mark 5:33). We may not wish to use the same methods. We could certainly benefit from their practice of sharing openly with one another.

What can we learn from this woman's story? We may ask which parts of this story relate to anything we ourselves have experienced, or ought to experience, in the Christian life. We can also cast our minds around to see if this account reminds us of others we have known or know. In terms of our mission it points to the importance of healing in our service to others. Yet it also underlines the fact that we have far more to offer than power which makes well. It is his peace which lies at the heart of everything else. Perhaps that is why Paul's formula for greeting those to whom he wrote letters was "Grace and peace."

1. Have you ever personally sensed God's power? What were the circumstances? How was this power recognized?

2. Do you ever tell God "the whole story" in prayer? What do you expect from this telling? What is your purpose in prayer?

3. How can you bring the peace of Jesus into other persons' lives? How can we help one another to find this peace through our fellowship together?

HARCOURT

One of the most prolific writers of Christian anthems in Nigeria was Harcourt White. He was a leper. A major world center for the cure and treatment of leprosy was Uzuakoli, in the eastern region of Nigeria. Harcourt White went there to be treated.

While there he met the famous leprosy doctor, Frank Davey. As well as being a medical man, he was also an ordained Methodist minister and a talented musician. Harcourt White had gone to Uzuakoli to be cured of leprosy. While there, however, he found far more. He learned the art of making and writing music, and he learned what it meant to be a disciple of Jesus Christ.

When he was adjudged to be cured, and qualified to receive the certificate to say so, Harcourt White chose to stay on and work among the leprosy patients. He also conducted and trained the choir at the chapel in the settlement. It was one way of saying his thanks for a much greater experience than he had expected.

9
JOHN THE BAPTIST
Luke 3:1-20

John the Baptist is described in all four Gospels (see Matt. 3:1-12, Mark 1:1-8, and John 1:19-28 for parallels of this story). Luke tells us about the respected secular and religious leaders of the day. In so doing he does not simply provide a context for John the Baptist's ministry. He is describing the soil in which the roots of that ministry were planted. Luke's mention of Tiberius the Roman Emperor, Pontius Pilate the governor of Judaea, and Annas and Caiaphas the high priests prepares for the radical confrontation between the spiritual message on the one hand and the social and political behavior of people on the other.

What do we know about John the Baptist? John had benefitted from a deeply spiritual heritage. The story of his conception by his mother Elizabeth (previously barren) and his father Zacharias, with the unusual decision about his name, is preceded by the beautiful story of the visit by Mary the mother of Jesus to the relative Elizabeth while both of them are pregnant. John was inheritor of a profoundly religious tradition. He may have lived among the Essenes, an ascetic (simple, rugged, self-denying) sect of Jewish religious men. Certainly his own lifestyle was ascetic in the extreme, as this passage shows.

Yet if this leads us to picture a somewhat mild and shy man, given to rather unrealistic spiritual ideas, we could scarcely be further from the truth. His message was plain, vigorous, earthy, and practical. Like the prophets of the Old Testament to whom Jesus was later to liken him, John called his fellows to repentance and baptism. He believed that the coming of the Messiah, the expected Anointed One of God, was drawing near. He therefore came singlehandedly to straighten the way for the Lord.

If Luke's first point is the sharpness of conflict between the spiritual and the socio-political outlooks, his second is that John's lifestyle exactly reflected his message. The desert place, symbolizing both the harshness of survival and the nearness to God of the prophets, chimed in exactly with his harsh words about people behaving like snakes, and about God coming like an axe to the trees, as well as with his call to his hearers to repent and be baptized.

When did John become a disciple of Jesus? The question is hard to answer since most of his short life was lived before Jesus' public ministry began. Indeed Jesus was to say that the least in the kingdom is greater than John the Baptist. Yet his loyalty to Jesus is abundantly clear in his task of baptizing the Lord. His heredity and family upbringing obviously helped. He was already in the desert when the word of the Lord called him to his ministry. He preached without fully understanding the implications of his message, as his encounter with Jesus over baptism clearly shows. But his later comments, about Jesus increasing while his ministry decreased, show how deeply committed to Jesus he was. He seems to have been a person in whose life both the long steady growth and the occasional sudden flashes of insight, matched by a willingness to act on what he understood, combined to produce a disciple.

What did John teach about discipleship? The message was undoubtedly a disturbingly spiritual one. Repentance means turning around. They are to leave their sins behind. They are also to be baptized, symbolic both of washing and of a total change of course in their life's intention. He expected inward change from his hearers.

But he also called for an outward transformation matching the inward attitude; a public change mirroring the private conversion. This would be reflected in generosity to the poor, justice at work, and honesty in dealing with others. John's grasp of the good news was rooted firmly in the soil of everyday life. He would not have understood modern distinctions between a spiritual gospel and a social gospel. He knew only the good news with deep inward roots of repentance and faith and observable external fruits of justice and peace.

This combination is clear, too, in his prophecy of the imminent coming of Jesus. Certainly he will baptize with the Spirit. By definition it is to be a spiritual experience. But it will be with the Spirit and fire. However inward and spiritual, the experience will also burn up any dross of wrong behavior in relation to others. The attitude John called for was equally expected from the high as from the low. John even criticized King Herod for his private life, and that was to prove fatal for John later.

What theology emerges from this story? There is first the theme of God's careful preparation for the coming of Christ. John the Baptist's privilege was to be the announcer that the time had come. Many before him had dreamed of the day, and longed for it in their own time. There is reference to this in 1 Peter 1:12, where we read that prophets were told how their work was for the benefit of others yet to come. To serve God involves taking the long patient view of the world's affairs. We are all, under pressure from the shortness of our time on earth, inclined to want things done quickly. But history takes time to make. Part of our cooperation in God's plans is to play our part faithfully and patiently, leaving the completion to God. Things completed in haste *are* often regretted at leisure. But there are moments of urgency and swift action, too, the culminating points of long preparation. John the Baptist had the privilege of playing his part in one such moment in history:

though he was eventually to discover how costly and painful such moments can be.

The second theological point concerns the place of justice in the purposes of God. John the Baptist's demands upon his hearers, in terms of how they should live their lives, are almost mundane. Giving a shirt away, collecting fair tax, not forcing people to do things against their will are each rather dull when contrasted with his earlier rhetoric about axes and roots and fires. But justice matters greatly in the kingdom of God. Mosaic law was meant to enshrine it. Kings were called to preserve it. Prophets were raised up to protest for it. A Christian or a church neglecting justice is ignoring a key principle of Old and New Testament Scripture.

Third, there is the significance of symbol—symbolic action and symbolic people. John's action in baptizing, plunging people beneath the water and raising them up through it again, symbolized far more than even he knew. Jesus' submission to baptism by John carries with it in our minds all the imagery of his own forthcoming death and resurrection. The symbol can often communicate what words cannot, and at a different level too. In this sense John was himself a symbol, his whole lifestyle communicating the urgency and the sharpness of God's call to prepare the way for the Messiah.

Yet words are needed, too. John tells his hearers what baptism means. He also tells them what he is doing. Words may stop short of symbol in the breadth of communication possible, but they are vital for precision and accuracy of understanding. We need symbol and word.

Fourth, there is the strange combination of good news and judgment, both coming from God. John is clear that to refuse the good news is to bring judgment upon oneself. His comments on Herod, and Herod's response, made that only too clear. There is a relentless battle between good and evil, truth and falsehood, requiring urgent commitment and wholehearted dedication.

Our Methodist tradition has not been good at handling some of these themes. We were born, as a movement, at a time of urgency in evangelism and growth. There was so much response that our style became pragmatic and reactive; dealing with issues as they arose, judging and being judged by the numbers who joined and by the spread of the Methodist societies. The regulations which govern Methodist church life today reflect that spirit of being structured for relentless action and growth. Our worship also carries the mood of our origins—instant, experiential, contemporary, offered to God in buildings which are essentially practical and utilitarian. Our calendars and diaries often reveal the frenzied activism of much of our Methodist life. Even our historical reflections are often better at telling the story than at learning its lessons. We may feel that other churches lack urgency and endeavor. We have to admit that we often lack patience and the capacity to be sustained by longer perspectives.

Neither are we very good at symbolism. In the eighteenth century the Methodist symbol was John Wesley himself! This part of our life is still reflected in the honoring of the President or Presiding Bishop, or Patriarch, in our various modern Methodist hierarchies. The nineteenth century development of British Methodism was marked by a move further away from symbolism, under the threat—as it was seen—of the Oxford Movement in the Church of England.

Methodism is better at justice! Our traditional alignment with lower social classes in many parts of the world has made us aware of how much injustice there is. A strong case can be made out to show that, alongside the centrality of evangelism and fellowship in eighteenth century Methodism, a strong reason for Methodist growth was the way in which members of the developing artisan class found their fulfillment within the Methodist system. They were growing in numbers and ability. Literacy was important for them, as was a forum for discovering a sense of purpose and expressing their views. In the Methodist societies they found these very things, literature to read, groups in which to articulate their views, even opportunities for leadership. They certainly did not receive total justice in the eighteenth century, but it is significant that Methodism has been criticized by the political left and praised by the political right for averting in England a revolution parallel to the French Revolution. Wesley addressed, in the name of the gospel, the cry of the artisan class for justice. We Methodists forget that at our peril.

This story therefore challenges us to be deeper in our discipleship, both spiritually and practically. It warns the church against trying to be spiritual or practical to the neglect of either emphasis. It calls us to reflect the message we preach in the lifestyle we adopt. It quickens us to recognize that there is no room in Christianity for "playing at church." We are engaged in activity which is ultimate and total. And we are given salutory evidence in John's story that we must be ready to pay the price of being true to our calling.

In particular, the story of John the Baptist's preaching is a sharp reminder that those who claim to have responded to the gospel must take seriously their commitment to justice for others. This is easy to see and act upon when some flagrant injustice is experienced by someone near us in a single incident. It is harder to perceive and to do anything when the people treated unjustly are at a distance from us or not known to us. It is most difficult of all when the injustice is built into the culture to which we belong, and yet we ourselves are not suffering. To do something about that is probably one of the most urgent challenges to Christians in the Western world.

Our questions for ourselves will therefore be about the oneness of our profession and our practice as Christians, individually and corporately. We will need to ask ourselves about the wrongs in the church and in the society which we ought to be addressing. Finally we may reflect on whether there are people we know who are going steadily down the wrong path, and who need our word of loving correction.

1. Is your approach to discipleship at this moment more "spiritual" or more "practical"? Give two examples of how you make this distinction.

2. Give one recent example of evil in your community. How can you confront or repair this evil?

3. What do you think of John's ascetic (strict, disciplined) lifestyle? Is it appropriate for today?

JIM

Jim Wallis was brought up within the Plymouth Brethren in the United States. As a teenager, however, he began to have doubts about the adequacy of the teaching being given. Not that Christian teaching was illogical or untrue within itself; rather it seemed to bear no practical relevance to the problems which were to him most pressing—the state of the poor, discrimination against black people, and the need for world peace. His elders in the church said they were concerned about these things. They even met, at Jim's request, a group of spokesmen for the black people. As one of the black leaders had warned him, the whites are willing to talk and promise, but they did not do anything. So it turned out.

Jim Wallis therefore broke from his church. He became very active in the Peace Movement, an organizer of the well-publicized marches across the country. His energies were now focused on those issues of great interest to him—the poor, the blacks, peace. Yet life was not well there, either. He found lacking a spiritual dimension. Not all who protested for peace were peaceful people. There was selfishness among those protesting for the poor. In a search for something deeper he turned to the Sermon on the Mount and found there the very thing that meant so much to him. He returned to the Christian fold, but not as he had left.

He founded, with the others, the Sojourner Movement. He lives in a community in Washington among the poor. He travels the world pointing out how the concern for peace, for the underprivileged and the poor, is at the very heart of biblical teaching and of the gospel. An uncompromising critic of hypocrisy and greed, he is for many a modern John the Baptist.

10
THE CENTURION
Luke 7:1-10

It is typical of Luke's Gospel to tell the story of a good Roman soldier. The Romans are viewed favorably in Luke's writings, along with the others whom first century Jews treated as less important or as enemies.

What do we know about the centurion? He is such a good man that Jewish people tell Jesus about him. He is kind to the Jews and actually built their synagogues. Apart from being a senior soldier, the centurion is a generous man with a warm heart toward the Jewish religion.

How did the centurion act? He has a servant who is sick. It appears typical of the centurion that he would be upset by a servant's illness.

What does the centurion know about discipleship? It is, perhaps, also typical of him that he will send for Jesus' help. Respect for the Jews must, in this case, have extended to include this exciting and disturbing new Jewish teacher. Whether because of particular admiration for Jesus, or because of urgency about his servant so that the nearest rabbi would do, the first step was his message to Jesus for help.

In general, it was not Jesus' custom to heal Gentiles. But Jews who know this man plead his cause. The second step, therefore, is when Jesus goes beyond his normal boundaries to meet a deep need in someone's life.

A third element now enters the story. The centurion is horrified to learn that Jesus is coming to his house to perform the cure. He himself knows what it is to have authority. He expects his commands to be obeyed instantly by the soldiers. If he holds such authority, he assumes that the divine authority of Jesus must be at least as good as that. The logic of his message to Jesus not to come to the house requires rather more than a perception of the nature of Jesus' authority, however. After all, the centurion needed to give his orders to his soldiers. Why wouldn't Jesus need to go to the house to heal the boy? The answer seems to be that the centurion had perceived what kind of war it was in which Jesus held such authority. It was a spiritual battle in which spiritual authority and weapons were required and where space and geographical location were less important. Time was important, however, since Jesus had so much to do urgently. So why waste the Master's time by taking him all the way to the house. If he says, "Be well!", it will be enough.

Evangelists are familiar with the phenomenon at the heart of this story. The Roman centurion is passing the ministry of Jesus through the only set of tests he knows how to apply. His life is dominated by war, discipline, authority, and victory. Jesus is fighting a war against evil in the spiritual realms. For this he plainly has authority, in view of the things the centurion knows he has already done. Over against a pastoral interpretation, where the shepherd naturally goes to the sheep in need, the centurion poses the picture of the military commander with no time to waste for such things. And the war is to be won. A word of command is all that will be necessary.

Many of us are so at home with this story that we miss the surprise which is built into the next step. Through knowing how much Jesus spoke of peace, we might have expected a total rejection of such a model for understanding his ministry. This is particularly to be expected since it came not only from a soldier but from a

Roman soldier. The surprise is that Jesus not only accepted this way of thinking but he actually praised it! "I have never found such faith as this, I tell you, not even in Israel!" (v. 9). Whether or not the centurion was using the best model for understanding Jesus, it is clear that it has given insight into the kingdom which others have missed. What is much more important, as Jesus' words show, it has provided an adequate vehicle for a deep faith which Jesus had not found among his Jewish compatriots. If only they had been able to believe in him as simply and totally as this centurion was now doing!

The surprise goes deeper. Luke says Jesus was himself surprised by this response from the centurion. He changes his plans in light of this development. Instead of going to the house, he simply responds to the centurion's message, and the servant is made well again.

What theological issues emerge from this story? In prime place is the cost of believing that the gospel is for all. We probably do not appreciate how difficult it was for Jesus, a Jew, to perform a miracle for a Roman centurion, a Gentile. Jews knew and felt themselves to be so much the special people of God. For Jesus to offer his grace to others was a most painful thing to do. Yet Jesus had before him evidence, as he himself said, of faith from a Gentile superior to anything he had found from Jews. How could God's grace not be for this man, too?

Then, second, the centurion used his own experience and setting to interpret the work of Jesus. If he, as a senior soldier, could give commands and be obeyed, how much more could Jesus. The theological point involved is profound. If the gospel, through Jesus, is for all in every culture, then it can be expected to call out a response from every culture. The universality of the message will be demonstrated in the universality of the answering voices of different cultures, places, and times. From Asia and Africa, the Americas,

Europe, and Pacific lands there will be a response to God's good news.

But it will not be the same response in detail, because the setting, experience, presuppositions, and perception of reality are not the same. The different responses from Jewish and Greek cultures in the early days of Christianity are clear in the pages of the New Testament. People are truly coming to God through Christ only when they bring their culture and experience with them. As they do so, new insights into the meaning of the gospel are discovered.

Of course it is the gospel which is the determining voice in this duet of call and response. In that sense all our culturally influenced responses must be tested for conformity to his call. But with that conformity there is room for much variety. African and Asian peoples, to whom the gospel was preached, understood the corporate ideas of the Bible much better than the Europeans who preached it to them. Each time the good news is taken to a new culture, those who take it must be prepared for the shock of seeing people respond out of their own cultural context, often in different ways from those intended by the bringers of the message.

The third theological insight focuses again on Jesus himself. The Gospels constantly force us again and again to ask, "What kind of person could do these things?" So here we are invited to ask, "What kind of person could respond to faith by declaring someone at a distance to be recovered from illness, and have the power to make it so?" Any interpretation of Jesus which leaves such questions unanswered is unsatisfactory.

The history of eighteenth century Methodism could be written as an exposition of this biblical passage. So much of it is really the story of what happens when new groups of people are introduced to living faith in Jesus Christ, as their own experience. Classes developed as units of pastoral care after leaders in the New Room, Bristol, discovered various needs among the membership while collecting one penny, per person, per week, from groups allocated to them. Meeting in classes and bands grew out of the late seventeenth and early eighteenth century practice of the self-improvement societies. Watchnight services and love feasts were partly an alternative attraction to the taverns, where some of the converts had previously spent a lot of their time. The Circuit system grew out of the need to care for large numbers of single societies, so that the preachers were Circuit preachers or riders. The practices varied and developed according to the usage as it extended.

All of this was sustained by an optimism of grace. If the gospel is for all then all must receive it, and they can only receive it as and where they are. Their growth in faith results from the interaction of the gospel truth with them in their culture and setting. The gospel message may not change as a result, for it is grounded once-for-all in Jesus' history. But our perception of it is deepened and widened as more cultures engage with it and bring their perspectives to it.

What lessons can we learn from the story of the centurion? First, concerning our own discipleship, we need to be sensitive about the degree to which our own cultural upbringing influences our understanding of the gospel in particular and the Bible in general. We may sometimes be propagating or defending truths which have more to do with our context than with the content of the message Jesus taught. We need help from each other in order to be sensitive.

Next we need to allow those coming into discipleship to bring with them their insights and perceptions. We should be careful not to force social, class, or cultural patterns on them in the name of Christianity. Those who have long been Christians have much to learn from those who are newly so.

Third, we need to ask whether our discipleship as a church is relating adequately to cultural change going on around us. Questions need to be asked about the music and liturgy in worship, about our organization and way of working, about the thought-forms and language with which we proclaim our gospel. We are not to be at the mercy of every whim of those around us, but we do need to be related enough to our cultural setting for real communication to be possible.

Finally, the story reminds us again that there is a divine power operating through Jesus. Christianity is not just about believing, serving, and working. It is also about *receiving*—about receiving divine power by the Holy Spirit to do all these things to which we feel called. We need faith like the centurion's as we trust in God's power in Christ to strengthen us.

We do well to be aware of how our own experiences inform our understanding of Jesus, how his impact upon us has changed our view of life's meaning, and how much we are willing to learn from our fellow Christians out of their rich pool of experience. It is as we learn in this way from one another that we are prepared for the kind of experience Jesus had with the outsider—to find someone exercising and expressing deep faith out of his or her own background. It may not be the way we would choose to understand or express it, but if it is God-given faith in Jesus, harmonious with the Jesus story, then we need to be able to welcome, nurture, and learn from it.

1. John Wesley's heart was strangely warmed at Aldersgate, so that he found personal assurance of God's grace. Have you ever experienced this personal warmth? If so, describe the episode in a few sentences.

2. In some cultures (and Christian denominations) God's grace is better understood from the New Testament as poured out on the community or people of God. Salvation is perceived and received as a group or church, much as Israel is elect in the Old Testa-

ment. Do you prefer this corporate view, or would you put more emphasis on the personal assurance?

3. What key elements in Jesus' story are central to the Christian message? Name at least three elements. How does Jesus' story interact with yours?

BILQUIS

Bilquis Sheikh is a Pakistani woman of noble birth. Her husband, then a high-ranking government official, left her. She returned to her family estate, living with her adopted grandson and surrounded by her servants, seeking peace. Somehow, it eluded her.

On one occasion a Christian missionary and his wife visited her. She thought them to be rather drab in their appearance, though pleasant and warm in their manner. Since reading the Koran failed to bring her the peace she needed, she asked one of her employees, whom she knew to be a Christian, to find her a Bible. He was obviously afraid of the consequences, and she had to press him a number of times before a Bible turned up in the house. She began to read both the Bible and the Koran, but was torn between the two.

One reason for her search was a sensation she had in her garden of a presence so tangible that she felt a touch on the arm. Another was a dream of having supper with a man she knew to be Jesus, then with another man she unaccountably knew to be John the Baptist. A second dream was of a perfume salesman offering her perfume glimmering like crystal. When she went to touch it he prevented her, saying, "This will spread throughout the world."

At some cost she consulted the missionary's wife who prayed with her and witnessed to her. When her grandson was ill she confided in a Roman Catholic nun, who was a doctor, telling her she was earnestly searching for God. The nun said, "Why don't you pray to the God you are searching for? Ask him to show you his way. Talk to him as if he were your father."

In many ways that was the turning point. At great cost Bilquis later committed her life to Christ, on the strength of unusual experiences and dreams, and of varied comments from different Christians. When she wrote the account of her conversion, she called it "I dared to call him father."

11
MATTHEW
Matthew 9:9-13

The Gospel of Matthew is associated with Matthew the tax collector, though there is a variety of opinion about what the link is. The connection does, however, give added significance to the brevity and modesty of the story of only five verses in which the call of Matthew (Levi the tax collector) is told.

There is almost an air of casualness about the episode. The call occurred as Jesus was walking along and came across Matthew at work. For Jesus, the call to discipleship was not something limited to special occasions. Any time was a time to face people with the realities of the kingdom, even people at work!

What do we know about Matthew? In Matthew's case the call at work has deeper meaning. Matthew's work made him the kind of person least likely to be invited by any Jew to join anything. He was a tax collector, helping the Romans to take money from his own people, and making a considerable profit out of it himself. He was responsible for work involving political, social, and religious betrayal of his kinsfolk. Why would anyone wish to call him to join the band of persons to introduce the new faith?

The brevity of the call and of the response perhaps hints at one answer to that question. It is easy to blame Matthew and his associates for the wrong they were doing. We need also to remember that they saw their opportunity in this new way of making money, they were decisive enough to take it on, and they were courageous enough to keep it going.

How did Matthew become a disciple? This capacity for instant, decisive action shows itself in Matthew's call. The story makes no allowance for his having heard Jesus, though no doubt the word about him was being passed around. Certainly in the story, as Matthew tells it, there is not even conversation, let alone preaching. Whatever the background knowledge he had, the strength of the call lay evidently in the nature of the call and the person who issued it. For a man of shrewd judgment, decisive action, and courage, Jesus' authority was all that was needed.

We may of course guess at more. Was he tired of the work he was doing, of the hypocrisy of a Jew cheating Jews, and of the greed which lay at its heart? Is it coincidence, for example, that it is Matthew who gives us the fullest account of the Beatitudes and the Sermon on the Mount, with their emphasis on inward quality and purity before God, issuing in right behavior in relation to others? Was he conscious of a growing guilt about the way he was living? Is it at least possible that this is one reason he seems readily and decisively to follow when called?

If so, then it is also surely significant that we have no hint that Jesus told him how wrong he had been and that he needed to repent. Neither did Jesus do so in the story of Zacchaeus, another tax collector. Zacchaeus brings up the issue of wrongdoing by promising to make restitution to all whom he had wronged. In Matthew's case it seems that the choice to follow Jesus—leaving the job behind and changing his lifestyle—was itself an act of both repentance and restitution. He didn't so much "say" his way into discipleship as "do" his way into discipleship.

The story does more. Through the call and response of Matthew, Jesus found a way into the company Matthew kept. Now it was Jesus whose ministry was judged by actions not words. This underlines the importance of making room in the kingdom for the "doing" people. By and large, people are less offended when we *say* the gospel words than when we *do* the gospel actions. In this story Jesus is criticized for going to eat with Matthew and his friends.

What theology lies within this story? Our Protestant emphasis on "salvation by faith alone" has rightly made us afraid of anything that looks like "salvation by works." A view of salvation based on works glorifies men and women rather than God. It also gives the kingdom to those of stronger will and energy. Religious systems based on what we do easily become idolatrous. Nevertheless, we must note that the dominance of the West in Christianity for centuries has overemphasized verbal articulation and conceptual grasp. It has overemphasized the power of the word and the idea at the expense of the action—doctrinal correctness at the cost of works of charity. In so doing, we have given the kingdom to the clever and voluble person, the theorist rather than the activist. Matthew's story may require us to realize that some people become and remain disciples by a series of "action-responses." They may not be able to talk about their faith, and some certainly could not describe it. Yet what they do is inspired by faith in God through Jesus, and on the strength of that faith they manage to be in the right place at the right time, doing the right deed. They may not speak their confession, talk about repentance, or testify to their faith. Yet what they do and the way they live reflect all three. The call of Matthew gives confidence to such people.

It was at this point of works in relation to faith that Wesley got out of step with many Protestants of his time, particularly the Calvinists. John Wesley's view of salvation as a whole followed Arminius more than Augustine in emphasizing the proper part played by human beings in putting their faith in Christ. We can only exercise faith because God's prevenient grace (grace which "comes before") enables us to do so, but we do exercise that faith. Wesley took the same line about holiness. He says that the works of the Christian are truly *his* works, though of course they can only be carried out because the Spirit enables them to take place. In teaching this, John Wesley was trying to avoid views of salvation which diminish human worth and personality. He wished to show that experience of salvation actually enhanced human works and personality, not least in our learning to walk in harmony with God so that our works truly honor him. Some Calvinists were not happy with this, fearing that it was a threat to salvation by grace through faith (that is, not through works) alone. Wesley actually held to that great Reformation slogan but argued that grace enables faith to perform its works so that they are truly our works and not a threat to the total operation of grace. Works could not happen without faith. Our works earn us no salvation; they are part of our experience of salvation.

Second, there is a theological point about the kingdom of God. The power of action to communicate meaning is revealed by Jesus. In going to eat with Matthew's associates, Jesus had raised, in a shocking way, the question of what the kingdom was about. There is an event needing an explanation. The kingdom is not about sending doctors to people who are well. It is the sick who need doctors. The irony is heavy. He had come to offer salvation to the religious Jews who were his brothers and sisters. Their leaders in particular, however, rejected what he offered. They did not judge themselves to need it. Jesus therefore tells them that he is going, as doctor, to those whom his critics certainly regarded as unwell: the religious outcasts of their society. "If you will not have me because you think you are spiritually healthy," Jesus is saying, "then let me go to those who have the sense enough to know that they are not spiritually healthy."

It must now be clear that this whole passage is not setting Christian actions in opposition to Christian words. Indeed it emphasizes the place for both. But without Matthew's response to Jesus' call and Jesus' response to Matthew's invitation, there would have been nothing to explain. This pattern of action and explanation lies at the heart of the Bible story. It is God's way of making himself known. The people of God would do well to copy his pattern.

What can we learn from this story? Maybe some who read this will be liberated by the assurance that being a Christian does not require us to be "good at talking." Our deeds can speak eloquently, too. Perhaps those who are good at words need to be sure that they do accept that not all Christians are talkers about their faith. What is equally clear, however, is that the Christian church as a whole needs to be characterized by deeds which are distinctive and words which explain the distinctiveness. The Christian church seems to oscillate between these two poles. There are periods when we concentrate on preaching and speaking so much that we do little in the world which requires our explanation. Then there is a swing of the pendulum in the other direction. Preaching and proclaiming become unpopular, and all the emphasis is on doing the works of the kingdom. In the first case, those outside listen in puzzlement as we answer questions they are not asking! In the second case they watch our deeds but find no answers to the questions they raise! Worst of all is the phase when each way of doing things has its champions, who fight one another over whether acting or speaking is more important. The biblical message suggests that both are vital, though their varying degrees of prominence may often be determined by the situation and the people involved, not by the preference of Christians for one or the other.

Two other points are raised, which we have seen in other stories. First, how surprising it must have been to the onlookers that Jesus would call an unpleasant man like Matthew to follow him. Jesus perceived the possibility of Matthew becoming a disciple when most others would have written him off as a traitor incapable of goodness. Second, note the limited amount of faith Matthew had when he started off as a disciple. This story seems to suggest that it does not matter *how much* faith he had. What does matter is that it was *faith in Jesus*. With faith in place, everything else would follow.

Yet for both of these things to be true and reliable, Matthew had to be impressed enough by Jesus himself to get up and follow. This was the focal point of his discipleship.

Today people often need merely to see Jesus in the lives of his disciples before they can consider discipleship to be possible for them. What we are helps or hinders them on their road to faith. We retain the combination of deeds and works in our Christian lives. As one American preacher put it, "What is it in your life that it takes Jesus to explain?"

1. Many people today have the same suspicion about politicians as Jews did about tax collectors. Can you, however, name a contemporary politician whose actions are inspired by faith through God in Jesus? Explain.

2. Describe two ways that you have been or could be a disciple of Jesus while at work or at school.

3. Jesus is a doctor for those who are considered spiritually unwell—in Matthew's case, the tax collector. In your community, with which outcasts would Jesus be associating? Do you minister to them as well?

BRIAN

One of the most feared groups in British and American society in the '60s and '70s was the Hell's Angels. They were groups of mostly young men and women who traveled on large, fast motorcycles, or motorcycles and sidecars. They dressed mainly in black leather outfits, and wore various military badges. There were different and competing groups. Each had its own set of rules, and its awards for various feats, most of them calculated to offend the general public. They often engaged in violent battles with one another, or with the police. Even today their presence in a neighborhood usually means trouble.

Brian was a Hell's Angel. As a result of his misdemeanors he ended up in prison for four years. During that time he was visited by the chaplain and by prison visitors. He received a Methodist newspaper and saw in one issue an advertisement for the Living Bible. He told the prison visitor he would like one.

When it arrived, and he read it, he was particularly gripped by the passage in John 15 where Jesus speaks of being the "vine," and tells his disciples to abide in him, and he in them. Brian had a deep inward sense of wanting to be fruitful in the rest of his life, yet knew it could only happen if he was truly given over to Jesus Christ, the vine.

In that commitment he finds his fruitfulness. Today he works with an inner-city Mission, engaged in Christian ministry.

12
PAUL
Acts 9:1-19

Paul is often regarded as the biblical focal point of evangelical religion. Indeed evangelicals have often rightly been accused of finding too many of their texts in Paul's letters and not nearly enough in the Gospels. It is, after all, Paul who sets out the great Christian doctrines of human sin, Christ's atoning death and resurrection, of the need for repentance, and conversion through saving faith into the experience of new birth and sanctification.

We might therefore expect the prime account of Paul's conversion to be a classic case along these lines, but it is not so. Paul's conversion focuses more on questions of action than of doctrine.

What do we know about Paul? We can read Philippians 3:4-6 for his own answer to the question. In this particular story he is on his way to Damascus to perform certain actions and executions. Because of his conviction that the Christian sect is a false and heretical one, he has decided to stamp it out. Other Jewish leaders thought that Christians were in error. Paul is the one who does something about it. He provides an example of radical obedience to deeply held convictions. What happened to him on the way to Damascus didn't change his commitment to radical obedience. It changed the basis of that obedience in a way which completely turned his life around. Whatever the form of the appearance of Jesus to him, it was evidently powerful enough to persuade him that he was altogether on the wrong track. All the zeal, clarity, and conviction he had brought to attacking the Christians must now be used in serving their Lord.

How did Paul become a disciple? In the first place, Paul is made dramatically aware of a power greater than his. Luke tells us in Acts that Paul had letters of authority for his task in Damascus. On the way, however, he is met by a different authority. This overpowering sense of divine power, enough to blind him, is the initial step in Paul's conversion. His own power and authority are put into the context of *divine* power and authority.

The second step is the identifying of divine power and authority with the Risen Christ. Paul had believed that the Christians were either totally misled or deliberately false. Now his own experience told him that they were neither. He had met the Risen Christ who stood at the heart of the Christian testimony. They were neither misled nor misleading. In other words, his overwhelming experience had some theological content to it. He had not only felt something, he had learned something also. In this sense it was a classic conversion—a change of mind and a change of heart.

Yet there is no mention of repentance, though no doubt Paul felt guilt for what he had done in persecuting the church. He certainly changed his mind, which is what repentance means. But he says no words about it. Neither is there any mention of Christ's atoning death. Nor is there reference to new birth or the gift of the Holy Spirit.

We may rightly conclude that Paul became aware of all these things during his years in retreat in Arabia. They are neither unrelated to his own experience nor out of harmony with it. But Luke gives no indication that these things were present in Paul's initial experience of conversion. Even Ananias' interpretation to Paul of what had happened to him is more about action than doctrine. It concerns his witness before kings and princes, and how much he must suffer for his testimony to Christ.

Paul does turn out to be a classic case of conversion after all, but not in the way we usually mean it. It is classic in the sense that he did not know all that was involved when he first became a Christian.

His experience began exactly where he was, expressing in action a deep conviction about religious truth. His experience gathered up the action based on deep conviction, but changed fundamentally the religious truth at its center. He had been persecuting the Risen Lord by attacking his people; now he must serve the Risen Lord by ministering to God's people and helping others to become people of God.

If by classic conversion we mean conviction of sin, declaration of repentance, affirmation of faith in the atoning death of Christ, and reception of the Holy Spirit in new birth, then a great deal is lacking from Paul's experience. The point here, however, is that the above account is not a classic conversion in the cases recorded elsewhere in the New Testament. Like Paul's experience here, the New Testament accounts of conversion have some of these elements, but only enough for genuine faith to be present.

What theology lies behind the story of Paul's conversion? First, we must notice how conversion for Paul meant a total turning. Although many of the elements associated with the classical evangelical conversion are missing, this central feature is there. Everything is going to be different after the Damascus Road experience. He had been viewing the Christians as his enemies; now they are his brothers and sisters. He had affirmed his Jewish faith with enthusiasm; soon he will be working to lead other Jews to faith in Christ. Something changed at the very center of his life when he acknowledged the risen Christ as his Lord. The implications of that change were to take a lifetime to work out, but his orientation was now wholly different. He was later to describe it as being "in Christ." His life from now on would be discontinuous from what had happened before, because he was now moving in a wholly different direction. Conversion introduces an entirely new compass setting for life's journey.

Yet the second theological point is that there was considerable

continuity, too. The God of redemption, who through Christ led
Paul to conversion, is also the God of creation who loves us and
shapes us before we come to faith. Paul's natural abilities and
characteristics were not left behind when he was converted. The
God of creation would use them in Paul's redemption experience.
His sharp mind and wide knowledge would now be used in defending and expounding the Christian faith. The zeal with which he had
persecuted the Christians would now be used, not in persecuting
opponents of Christianity but in telling them of God's love in Jesus.
God takes us as we are, and makes what we are into disciples of
Jesus. Of course we have to leave some things behind. A converted
murderer or thief is not likely to need those skills in the kingdom of
God! And the way we use our knowledge and abilities is often
changed, too. But we remain ourselves, and what we are is important. It is a mistake to think that honoring Christ somehow means
turning ourselves into insipid, incapable people needing constantly
to be held upright by God. Rather, conversion is meant to lead us
into a robust offering of all our gifts and graces in divine service, so
that we and they are cleansed, quickened, and made whole.

The third theological point relates to the absence of reference to
repentance, or Christ's atoning death, to mention only two elements often proclaimed by evangelists. This raises a very large issue
indeed. Here we may suggest that, although in the New Testament
church there was an agreed content to the gospel message, all
the message was not necessarily preached every time evangelism
took place. Compare Paul's address on Mars Hill in Athens (Acts
17:22-31), with what he says he preached at Corinth, where he went
directly from Athens (1 Corinthians 2:1-5; for the link between the
two see Acts 18:1). He had converts at both places, but his message
was not the same. The reason for the difference was probably the
people he preached to and the circumstances he faced. Under God's
guidance he spoke to people about those parts of the gospel message most directly related to their situation and need.

Since audiences did not always hear the full message preached, it is not surprising that they professed faith without understanding the whole message. Faith as the way into discipleship in the New Testament is not primarily dependent on intellectual grasp of a wide range of concepts. It is rather, and here intellectual grasp will play a large part for some people, a case of perceiving enough to be willing to commit one's life to God in Christ. What we do not understand, when we first commit our lives to Christ, we can learn within the fellowship of his people, the community of believers. The question for the beginning of the Christian life is therefore not whether we understand the whole message but whether we perceive enough to commit ourselves by faith. We spend the rest of our lives on earth, and beyond, discovering the implications.

The fourth theological insight is something which Paul learned on the Damascus Road. Paul was on his way to Damascus to persecute Christians. He found out on the road that to attack Christians was to attack Jesus Christ himself. The question he faced from the risen Lord was not, "Why do you persecute my people?", but "Why do you persecute me?" (Acts 9:4). The risen Lord truly is at the heart of God's people, however small or humble their congregation or their premises may be. Such an insight should encourage us to think and speak of the church with much greater affection, and to work within it with much greater awe; it is his Body.

Our Methodist history and theology gathers into itself a number of these points. One thinks of the way in which many of the early Methodists, from very humble origins, not only had their natural abilities used in Methodism but actually discovered capacities for service that they did not think they possessed! The leaders themselves, especially John and Charles Wesley, brought immense ability with them into the faith, abilities stemming from their heredity and their upbringing. These were all used in God's service once the central release had taken place.

In terms of Christ's presence among his people, the early Methodists, in bands and classes, were sustained by this reality. Often at odds with or unwelcome in the local parish church (and the blame is not on one side), they found their integrity and worth in the presence of their Lord only in small fellowship groups. However little or much they understood when they became Christians, the bands and groups, the love feasts and the watchnight services were their arena for learning the implications of that crucial step of commitment to Christ.

What can we learn from Paul's Damascus Road experience? If we begin with the nature of Paul's experience, we cannot avoid the fact that his conversion had a good deal to do with action as well as attitude. Ananias was instructed to tell Paul that he was to witness to Gentiles, to kings, and to the people of Israel for the sake of Jesus. And Paul was to suffer for doing so (Acts 9:15-16). We need to recognize that the form of that witness varies today, from place to place and person to person. For some it is to preach, as Paul was to do. For others it is to hold high office and responsible jobs, and to witness by the quality of their lives and work, as well as by their words. For others it will be to protest to those in authority about the injustice and poverty in society. Yet others will be found caring for the needy and the helpless. For all, as for Paul, it will mean that attitudes changed by faith must be reflected in actions directed by faith.

Second, we may notice that those who seem furthest away from us may not be as far away as we think. Paul's threatening activity toward Christians reflected his restless search for truth and perfection. He found the clue in Jesus. Why do some atheists spend so much time telling us why there is no God? They do not believe a deity exists, yet they seem unable to leave God alone!

Third, we can see that if people do have a sudden moment of commitment, as some do, it depends on a great deal that has gone before, and on a great deal that is yet to happen. Paul's Damascus Road experience was prepared for by much thought and activity, and probably by his witnessing Stephen's triumphant martyrdom (Acts 7:58). Damascus Road was a culmination of many other events. It was also the foundation for many more. Paul needed to be helped into Damascus (Acts 9:8-9), to be visited by Ananias (Acts 9:10-19), to learn what the faith was about (1 Corinthians 15:3-11). So we can expect God to be at work in the lives of others, even if we cannot see it happening. And when people become disciples of Jesus they need help to grow in understanding, in faith, and in action for Christ.

The wholeness of our salvation does not, in the end, depend upon the extent of our knowledge. It depends upon the faithfulness of God who gives us salvation. We want to know more because God is so good, and because the more we know the deeper our experience of the faith can be. It is this progress or maturity which our conversion, our beginning on the way of discipleship, is truly about.

Believing and doing is a pattern for discipleship and growth. We are not identical in the faith that brings us in or in our process of growth. But we are all working toward a wholeness for which we will need one another.

1. Some Christians say, "God is Love. That's all we can be sure about." In light of Paul's initial experience with the Risen Lord on the Damascus Road, do you think that this is all the young Christian can know and experience with certainty?

2. Why is it that Christians often become immediately active upon first experiencing God's love and then shift their passion away from *doing* God's work?

3. Discuss whether it is appropriate to feel guilty if you are *being* Christian rather than an *acting* Christian.

ADAM

Adam is Polish and an ordained Methodist minister. As a boy he grew up within a Methodist church but, like so many, he became less and less keen about it. He was politically aware, however, and as a young man he was taken away by the police from the supper table at his home.

As he rose, unwillingly, his father pushed a New Testament in Polish into his hands. He took it in the commotion, but he had no desire for it. In prison, however, he soon found himself reading it more and more, and being sustained by its messages. One night he was taken for interrogation, and part of the pressure upon him was the steady tearing up of his New Testament page by page. Some pages were used to light cigarettes through the long night of questioning.

When he was finally sent back to his room, he was made to clear the snow outside. There, in the snow, was a New Testament, in Russian. To this day he does not know who put it there, though he has his suspicions. But why in Russian? He knew the answer later when he was drafted into the Russian army and could use his Testament to witness to Christ. God had called him that he might tell the good news, at considerable personal cost, in some strange places. So it has continued to be.

13
THE PHILIPPIAN JAILOR
Acts 16:16-34

For the Philippian jailor the day described in Acts 16 probably began like every other day. How different it was to be before it ended!

Who was the Philippian jailor? As with so many New Testament people, we actually know very little about this man. He was a jailor. This means that he was probably a retired soldier. We learn from the story that he was a husband and a father, since Luke refers to all his family being baptized (Acts 16:33-34).

What kind of person was the jailor? As a military man now entrusted with a prison, he was obviously disciplined and trustworthy. Compassion was not high on his list of qualities, however. After accepting men who had received "a severe beating" (Acts 16:23), and whose wounds needed bathing (Acts 16:33), the jailor put them into the inner cell and fastened them into the stocks. His task was to have prisoners safe and available when next they were needed. He could evidently be relied upon to do that without scruple.

We also can see that he was an honorable man. When he discovered that the doors were open and the prisoners loose, he assumed that they had already escaped (Acts 16:27). In that setting, having failed in his duty, the former soldier decided he must do the only proper thing and take his own life. He had betrayed his charge and no longer deserved to live. We are dealing, therefore, with a man of honor.

How did the jailor become a disciple? Of all the people in our studies, this man did least in seeking faith. In fact he did nothing! He did not set out to persecute the Christians as such, as Paul had done on the Damascus Road (Acts 9). He was not even in a context where Jesus could be expected to appear, as Matthew was (Matthew 9). He was simply minding his own business and doing the job he was paid to do. He must not lose his prisoners, whoever they were and whatever they professed to believe. His treatment of them relates to that simple duty alone.

What happened next was in no sense his responsibility. Incredibly, the prisoners in the inner cell were praying and singing hymns (Acts 16:25). Then there was an earthquake. Luke tells us that the prison foundations shook, the doors sprang open, the chains broke apart, and the prisoners were free. By the time the jailor got to the scene, having himself been awakened by the earthquake, he assumed the prisoners had escaped, and prepared to kill himself.

He discovered, however, that he was not the only person who knew about discipline. The prisoners had not run away, partly for reasons given later in the story (Acts 16:35-40). Paul discouraged him from harming himself. In face of such self-control and compassion the jailor asked, "What must I do to be saved?" They tell him to "believe in the Lord Jesus." They also "preached the word to him." His response is shown in two different ways. First he bathed their wounds, an act of compassion for them, matching theirs for him in not running away. Second, he submitted to being baptized by them, he and his family. He washed the dirt from their wounds; they washed the dirt from his soul (Acts 16:33). His family shared his faith, and therefore they shared the baptism and the joy (Acts 16:34).

What theology is indicated by this jailor's story? There is first something about God's sovereignty as experienced both by the disciples and the ones who became disciples. God's way of ruling the world is neither simple nor predictable. It is complex and often defies our capacity to forecast what will happen. It is not inconsistent, as though God were self-contradicting. There are principles at work, and these principles are related to and dependent upon the internal nature of God. God is loving, true, just, creative, redeeming, and fulfilling. But we cannot always understand why God does certain things in our lives, or what God will do in our lives. One reason is that God is committed, as the life, death, resurrection, and ascension of Jesus demonstrate, to work out the divine will in the midst of the circumstances of everyday life.

God does not leave us to get on with life without a presence or help. The Old Testament writers portrayed this characteristic in very homely terms, as though God were personally responsible for each change in the weather. It was their way of affirming the divine presence. Yet neither does God manipulate us by superior power, so that we become less than human beings created in God's image. The Creator intends us to be free in our choices and our goodness. The Redeemer knows that we cannot be saved apart from God. The result is a complex tangle of interrelated events and influences in which divine love patiently works for our good and the good of the world which God gives us.

We see this clearly in the case of Paul. He was himself fully involved in all that happened. There might have been no trouble at all. He could have ignored the slave-girl's remarks. When faced with a beating, he might have apologized and gone free. After the earthquake he could have run away. At each point there was a choice to be made, by Paul and the other Christians on one side, and by the owners, the authorities, and the jailor on the other. God's sovereignty is worked out by participation within that complex interaction of events. A moment's reflection on our own lives will reveal how true that is. God is neither absent from the details of daily living nor is God controlling them like some computer operator. God is personally involved in and with them, as Jesus showed in his ministry. Our response must be like that of Paul and his companions in this story: to discern moment by moment, according to what we know of God through Jesus, what we can best do next in harmony with God's will. This approach will cause us to be less concerned to puzzle about why things happen to us, and more concerned to ask what good can come out of them.

A similar challenge faced the jailor himself. Certainly the unexpected had overtaken him. Certainly the suicide path was a normal one if he had failed. But since the prisoners were all still there, he could easily have secured them again, grateful that they had not had the sense to run at the first opportunity. Instead he came to Paul and Silas and asked how he could be saved.

We cannot be sure why he chose that way. It could be that the link between the earthquake and the opening of doors and breaking of chains was acknowledged by him as of divine origin. It may be that he had heard the testimony of the fortuneteller to Paul and Silas: "They announce to you how you can be saved!" (Acts 16:17). He may also have been impressed by these men, and not least by their using the time in prison for praying and hymn singing. Whatever the reasons (and they could be different from any of these), in the complicated tangle of events he perceived the opportunity to seek salvation, and in so doing he found it, he and his family.

A second theological point concerns salvation by grace and its implications for Christian witness. Some of us are very familiar with the idea that salvation by grace is a way of making plain that the person entering into salvation does not earn that right. But there is another implication, and it is for those who are the witnesses to salvation by grace. Just as those who receive grace cannot earn it, so those who are messengers of that grace cannot control it. Paul deals with that point in 1 Corinthians 1:18-31, where he contrasts the many words of human wisdom and the one (gospel) word of divine wisdom; where he contrasts the worldly desire for miracles and wise thought with the "foolish message we preach,"

the message of Christ crucified. Alongside that theological argument
he goes on to describe the circumstances in which he preached this
message: "So when I came to you I was weak and trembled all over
with fear, and my teaching and message were not delivered with
skillful words of human wisdom, but with convincing proof of the
power of God's spirit" (1 Corinthians 2:3-4). He was so patently an
instrument of God's grace precisely because he came to them alone
and fearful. If they were impressed, it was not with him but with the
message. The result was, "Your faith, then, does not rest on (human)
wisdom but on God's power" (1 Corinthians 2:5).

The same thing happened in the story of the Philippian jailor. Paul
and Silas could hardly have been weaker—beaten, imprisoned, in
stocks. Yet as they prayed and sang their hymns, God's power was
made plain. We may recall how many of God's servants, in Old and
New Testaments, appeared to be not very good candidates in their
own right to do what God called them to do. Most of all, we will
remember that Jesus became the means of our salvation precisely
through the "weakness" of dying on the cross. This is probably why
Paul felt able to write that when he prayed to the Lord to remove what
he calls his "thorn in the flesh," the reply he got was, "My grace is all
you need; for my power is strongest when you are weak" (2 Corinthians 12:8-9). Paul can write, a little later in the same letter, "For when I
am weak, then I am strong" (2 Corinthians 12:10).

In Methodist terms "the triumph of grace" is almost a summary of
the history of the eighteenth century development. In many ways
John and Charles Wesley and a few of their friends were isolating
themselves from the church which they loved in order to reach the
masses whom they believed the church to be neglecting. They were
criticized and persecuted for it. The local leaders and, increasingly,
the preachers were taken from the ranks of the partially educated
and the uneducated. They had no buildings and no initial organization. Almost everything depended, humanly speaking, on the leadership of John Wesley, whose own frailties in terms of human re-

lationships were at times only too obvious. An Oxford don leading a mixed band of artisans and others is hardly a recipe for success. But they were committed to the working of grace and—against the gloomy perspectives of some Calvinists—to the optimism of grace. From day to day they went tenuously forward, but in their weakness God's strength was more plain.

What are we to learn from these things? First, we must surely reflect that the work of making disciples is God's more than it is ours. That is not to say that we have little to do, but it is to say that God's part and power are far, far greater. If we forget that, we easily become too proud in success and too depressed in failure. We attach too much importance to outward factors—organization, methods, publicity, speakers, and words. We pay too little attention to the hidden elements—the power of prayer, the work of the Holy Spirit, the mysterious event of new birth, and the battle between good and evil in the spiritual realm. We begin to think of it as our mission, rather than as our part in God's mission. We become too committed to forms of evangelism with which we are comfortable, and not ready enough to change in obedience to God's will. In the end we ourselves become the focal point of mission, whereas the two focal points are God and the world God loves.

The second lesson follows naturally. Our very weakness is often the avenue God uses to demonstrate divine power. I do not mean that we should somehow make ourselves weak by deliberately organizing badly, not preparing our sermons, or being careless about our witness. I mean, rather, that in face of the enormous task of leading men and women to faith in Christ we should recognize our weakness, but not be discouraged by it. Another implication is that those of us (and we may all fit into this category) who feel ill-equipped to speak about our faith to others should rather be encouraged to believe that through our weakness God can work to lead another to faith. The same applies to churches as to individuals.

The third implication is that we will not be able to understand everything that happens to us day by day. Life is too complex, and God's sovereignty too profound, for that. But we can accept what God gives, and our proper part in it, each day as an experience of harmony with the divine will. And we can seek rather to ask, not why this has happened but what good may come out of it. It is another way of affirming one of John Wesley's favorite sayings, "The best of all is, God is with us."

1. Do you think that God is involved in the affairs of the world in general and your life in particular? What evidence would you give?

2. What do you think Paul meant when he said, "When I am weak, then I am strong"? Can you describe an episode when your weakness or failure was blessed by God? How would the mission of the church be stronger if Paul's statement were put into practice?

3. The Philippian jailor discovered that Paul and Silas did not behave as prisoners usually did. He could therefore ask for their help about salvation. What differences in behavior should people see in us if we expect the same thing to happen?

CHUCK

Chuck was a member of the inner group around Richard Nixon when he was President of the United States. As a former U.S. marine, and a lawyer, he was particularly known for being a very strong, even ruthless man. All of this he placed at the disposal of the President. When the Watergate scandal became public news it was clear that Chuck Colson was implicated. All the power and authority he had possessed were suddenly taken from him.

Before his trial he visited a longstanding friend and noticed a great change in his attitude and behavior. The man told him that he had become a Christian. Chuck visited him again and eventually committed himself to Christ. He was sent to prison after his trial and there met with a few fellow prisoners for Bible study and prayer. He has since founded the Prison Christian Fellowship. In telling his story to the World Methodist Council at Nairobi in Africa, Chuck Colson said that he was deeply moved by the fact that after all the power he had held, it was in his weakness that Jesus met him, and that it was his weakness which Jesus used.

How to Finish This Book

In one sense only you the reader can reach new conclusions. Groups who have used this book as a study source might like to write their own conclusions after this study of Christian disciples.

Three elements involved in becoming a disciple may be seen in a slightly different light as a result of your examination of the set passages. The elements are repentance, belief, and new birth.

Repentance comes from a Greek word meaning a change of mind or purpose. It is often used in Christian preaching in connection with a feeling of guilt because of sin. For many persons this is the basic awareness as they give themselves by faith. Certainly our commitment of our lives to God in Christ will involve a change of mind and purpose, partly because we are not satisfied with our life as it is, in its sinful nature. But the point of our studies, and therefore the point for our hearing or sharing the good news, is that a sense of sin may not be the major reason we "change our mind and purpose" in response to the gospel. At the time your focus may be on reaching out for something better, rather than on the awfulness of what now is. In such cases the real awareness of sin and its consequences comes later.

The second constant element, and easily the most significant in the stories we have studied, is belief. Certain things must now be clear. One is that the degree of our belief, the amount of faith, is not nearly so important as the object of our faith, God revealed in Jesus. Faith like a grain of mustard seed *is* enough, so long as it is faith in Christ.

Another striking feature of many of the stories is how little people knew or understood when they committed themselves. It was enough that they genuinely wished to "turn around" and that Jesus Christ was the reason. All the learning lay ahead according to their own needs. The way to faith and the maturing of faith was so clearly in harmony with the kind of people they were. Grace found them where and as they were, and faith sprang like a shoot out of that soil.

The third major element in many stories can be described as new birth. Jesus commended this particularly to Nicodemus (John 3), but in its broadest sense it is present in most stories. If repentance is about changing mind and purpose, that is, turning around; and if belief is about finding a new focal point for life, that is, Jesus Christ; then new birth is about making a fresh start, that is, setting off in a new direction in service of Christ. In literature generally in the first century it was used as a new beginning in history, the inception of some new era; or of horticulture, with some new flower or fruit; or of personal life with some important new stage. At its heart lies Jesus' teaching to Nicodemus about the work of the Spirit, unseen yet powerfully present. New birth is dependent upon the inner work of the Spirit in the life of the believer. Its effect is a new beginning, and this is expressed in our New Testament stories in a variety of ways. For Matthew it was to leave his work and follow Jesus; for the paralytic to be up and walking; for the Philippian jailor to make his testimony and treat prisoners differently. However it showed, the change was evident.

Repentance, belief, and new birth are not the only elements present. And they are in any case present to different degrees in different stories. Any sharing with others on the strength of these studies must have revealed how true that is for us today. None of us can impose on others one pattern of becoming, or being, a disciple. All our views are too narrow unless they are informed or enlarged by the perspectives of the whole of Scripture and by the experiences of other Christians. If this book helps that process forward, then it ought also to quicken our desire to help others become disciples.